GO TO GALILEE

Go to Galilee

The Spiritual Geography of the Gospels

Sr. Virginia Marie Butler, OP

ALBA·HOUSE   NEW·YORK

SOCIETY OF ST. PAUL, 2187 VICTORY BLVD., STATEN ISLAND, NEW YORK 10314

ST PAULS

New Testament citations from *The New Testament: St. Paul Catholic Edition* (New York: Alba House, 2000).

Library of Congress Cataloging-in-Publication Data

Butler, Virginia Marie.
    Go to Galilee : the spiritual geography of the Gospels / Sr. Virginia Marie Butler.
        p. cm.
    ISBN 0-8189-0887-4
        1. Jesus Christ—Journeys. 2. Bible. N.T. Gospels—Geography. 3. Christian life.
    4. Palestine—Description and travel. I. Title.

    BT303.9.B88 2001
    226'.091—dc21

                                                                00-052594

Produced and designed in the United States of America by the
Fathers and Brothers of the Society of St. Paul,
2187 Victory Boulevard, Staten Island, New York 10314-6603,
as part of their communications apostolate.

ISBN: 0-8189-0887-4

Printing Information:

Current Printing - first digit   1   2   3   4   5   6   7   8   9   10

Year of Current Printing - first year shown

2001   2002   2003   2004   2005   2006   2007   2008   2009   2010

DEDICATED TO
The memory of
Sister Mary James Carroll, OP

But if the while I think on thee, dear friend,
All losses are restored and sorrows end.

William Shakespeare
Sonnet XXX

Table of Contents

Acknowledgments

I would like to thank my Dominican Congregation of St. Catherine de' Ricci (Elkins Park, PA) for the opportunity of extended study in the Holy Land — an experience that gave me a whole new understanding of Sacred Scripture and inspired the writing of this book. I am equally grateful to Catholic Theological Union, Chicago, for its uniquely rich program of study and exploration in the lands of the Bible.

My gratitude extends as well to Carolyn Osiek, RSCJ, who critiqued the earliest draft of my work and wrote back to me, "Yes, I think you might be able to publish this." And to Mary Terese Donze, ASC, for teaching me to "edit out every unnecessary word" and who shielded me against discouragement by showing me her file of literary rejects. Each of these authors encouraged me more than they know.

Biblical Abbreviations

OLD TESTAMENT

Genesis	Gn	Nehemiah	Ne	Baruch	Ba
Exodus	Ex	Tobit	Tb	Ezekiel	Ezk
Leviticus	Lv	Judith	Jdt	Daniel	Dn
Numbers	Nb	Esther	Est	Hosea	Ho
Deuteronomy	Dt	1 Maccabees	1 M	Joel	Jl
Joshua	Jos	2 Maccabees	2 M	Amos	Am
Judges	Jg	Job	Jb	Obadiah	Ob
Ruth	Rt	Psalms	Ps	Jonah	Jon
1 Samuel	1 S	Proverbs	Pr	Micah	Mi
2 Samuel	2 S	Ecclesiastes	Ec	Nahum	Na
1 Kings	1 K	Song of Songs	Sg	Habakkuk	Hab
2 Kings	2 K	Wisdom	Ws	Zephaniah	Zp
1 Chronicles	1 Ch	Sirach	Si	Haggai	Hg
2 Chronicles	2 Ch	Isaiah	Is	Malachi	Ml
Ezra	Ezr	Jeremiah	Jr	Zechariah	Zc
		Lamentations	Lm		

NEW TESTAMENT

Matthew	Mt	Ephesians	Eph	Hebrews	Heb
Mark	Mk	Philippians	Ph	James	Jm
Luke	Lk	Colossians	Col	1 Peter	1 P
John	Jn	1 Thessalonians	1 Th	2 Peter	2 P
Acts	Ac	2 Thessalonians	2 Th	1 John	1 Jn
Romans	Rm	1 Timothy	1 Tm	2 John	2 Jn
1 Corinthians	1 Cor	2 Timothy	2 Tm	3 John	3 Jn
2 Corinthians	2 Cor	Titus	Tt	Jude	Jude
Galatians	Gal	Philemon	Phm	Revelation	Rv

Something to Get You Started

One of the best known and respected Scripture scholars of the twentieth century was Sulpician Father Raymond E. Brown (1928-1998). His entire adult life was dedicated to biblical study and research, and to writing and lecturing on the meaning of God's Word. Yet, for all his academic pursuits and achievements, Father Brown acknowledged that his discovery of the Bible's treasures had come not through school courses but from his own reflective reading of the sacred texts. He was convinced, therefore, that "with a little effort people can become fascinated by the Scriptures. But," he added, "something needs to get them started."

This book offers one such "something" that came to me during an extended study program in the Holy Land. Earlier studies had long since claimed my enthusiasm for the Bible and led me, happily, to sharing God's Word through the ministry of retreats and teaching. But something more happened as I sojourned in the land of the Bible. I had expected to be as deeply moved as I was by the experience of living and travelling in the very places where Jesus lived and died and rose from the dead. What I had not anticipated was the effect of the land itself on me and consequently on the way I began to read and understand the Scriptures, beginning with the Gospels. Our study group had travelled on the Sea of Galilee and throughout its surrounding plains and rolling hills; we climbed mountains and descended into deep caves; we crossed deserts in daytime heat and in nighttime chill. Through these varied terrains the road continually unfolded before us, leading us always and finally to Jerusalem, the city of Jesus' destiny. One could not help but be struck by the symbolism of this physical geography for Christian life and spirituality.

If further impetus for pondering this concept was needed, it seemed to come every time I opened my Bible. Reading the gospels was now like continuing my pilgrimage through a land I had been travelling all along. It was meeting Jesus again and again in the familiar terrains of my own life's journey. Yes, I had studied, loved and taught Sacred Scripture — but now, in a new and real way, the Bible became *my* story as I read and pondered it in my heart through the medium of the land.

Returning to ministry at the conclusion of this study experience, I have been delighted to find that "reading the land" is an exciting and effective way for interested adults to become fascinated with Scripture — whether they have visited the Holy Land or not. This is because we can travel through the same changing landscape whenever we read the Bible. There the Judeao-Christian tradition of God at work in human history is woven from three strands: the people, the land and the Bible itself. The three come together for us precisely because of the

Book, for the Book is the living memory of the people of the land. Could our God have conceived any simpler way for us to sojourn at will in the Land of Promise, in the Land of Fulfillment?

Because the Bible is a book of faith, it is through faith that we must approach it — whatever means we use to get us started. Accordingly, *Go to Galilee*'s theme emerges from the most basic traditions of Christian faith: that Jesus suffered, died and rose from the dead (1 Cor 15:3,4); and that you and I can rejoice in resurrection only when we come to terms with the cross in our lives (Mk 8:34). The opening chapters serve to reground us in these central truths of faith and prime us for our journey with a surprising new insight about what was communicated from the empty tomb of Christ. The Easter message now becomes both a personal invitation and a compelling challenge to travel the biblical landscapes. The remaining chapters lead us through the changing terrain wherein we readily recognize the familiar patterns of our own spiritual journey and, through the power of God's Word, discover new depth of meaning in all of life's happenings. Gradually, we come to a rich understanding of what Saint Paul meant when he said: "The word is near you, in your mouth and in your heart" (Rm 10:8).

With its intention of motivating people toward their own fascinating study of Scripture, this book asks its readers to open their Bibles looking not for meaning, clarification, answers or proofs. Rather, it invites them to tap into the creative and intuitive qualities of faith that characterize the four Gospel accounts. It encourages them to use their imaginations to capture the spirit of the Bible — or, rather, to allow its spirit to capture them. In fact, *Go to Galilee* suggests an approach to Scripture modelled on that of Mary who received God's Word into her heart, pondered it there and acted upon it in her everyday life. In the same way for us, the seed of God's Word is sown into our hearts, grows as we reflect on it in our lives, and develops into the fruit of a personal spirituality of our own. For spirituality is simply how we live and pray our belief in God. To have a spiritual sense of life is to find meaning and direction in the events, places, people and circumstances of one's own life, for it is through these encounters that we perceive God at work in us.

It has been my privilege over the years to meet and work with many deeply spiritual men and women. These have been professionals, students, working folk of all ages, married and single — "just ordinary people," they would say. *Go to Galilee* is written with just such ordinary people in mind. I hope and believe it will provide enough of a start for them to put forth the little effort necessary to become eager students of God's Word to them and about them.

Virginia Marie Butler, OP

Elkins Park, Pennsylvania

Part One

This Is Our Faith

1

Sitting There, Facing the Tomb

Don't you know that those of us who were baptized into Christ Jesus were baptized into his death? Therefore, we were buried with him through our baptism into his death, so that, just as Christ was raised from the dead by the Father's glory, we too might be able to lead a new life. (Rm 6:3, 4)

Among those who walked with Jesus as he toured all of Galilee, some had been friends and neighbors of his family in Nazareth where he grew up. Most had come to know him only more recently when, after the arrest of John the Baptist, he began to preach publicly: "The appointed time has come and the Kingdom of God is at hand; repent and believe in the good news!" (Mk 1:15).

Jesus' reputation had spread quickly throughout Galilee and the surrounding region — mainly because of his healing power. The report was that he cured people of disease and illness of every sort and that even those possessed by evil spirits had been set free at his command. The crowds who followed him, therefore, were largely people seeking cures for themselves or bringing others to be healed. Besides these were many who came to satisfy their curiosity.

But there was also a small, growing number who felt their hearts moved more by what he said than by what they had seen him do. These not only heard but listened — and for them his words had authority such as they had never sensed in the scribes who were the official authorities on the law and traditions. This was a new kind of teaching and they were completely spellbound by the teacher (Mk 1:22; Mt 7:28, 29; Lk 4:32).

His closest friends were the Twelve — the men Jesus himself had chosen to be with him in community and ministry (Mk 3:13-19) — and the women who accompanied him throughout Galilee and who went with him on his final journey up to Jerusalem (Lk 8:1-3; Mk 15:41).

From the outset, there had been a sense of foreboding about this Passover pilgrimage. Jesus' growing popularity with the people was a matter of concern for religious leaders and government officials alike. His companions had heard rumors of plots against him and on more than one occasion, the Master had taken them aside privately and spoken as though to prepare them for approaching trouble. Although his meaning remained obscure to them, his words were serious and his manner grave. Nevertheless, he went ahead with his ascent to Jerusalem where his ministry continued.

After Jesus raised Lazarus from the dead, many more people believed and came to the Temple daily to listen to him, hanging on his every word (cf. Lk 19:48). The chief priests, scribes and leaders of the people became nervous and fearful: "If we leave him like this, everyone will believe in him" (Jn

11:48). Together they determined to find a way to silence him. Their opportunity came through one of his own when Judas, for a price, offered to deliver Jesus into their hands. Judas knew that after their Passover meal Jesus and his companions would leave the city, cross over the Kidron Valley and climb the Mount of Olives, passing through a garden place called Gethsemane. The conspirators were to position themselves at the garden's edge and, at the betrayer's sign, move in to make their arrest. It happened just so and in the scuffling and confusion that followed, the disciples "all abandoned him and fled" (Mk 14:50; Mt 26:56). Jesus was seized and led away.

Word of Jesus' arrest reached the women as he was being led during the night first to Caiaphas, next to Pilate, then to Herod. By early morning, they were following through the narrow streets as Jesus was being returned by Herod's soldiers to Pilate. They witnessed him being bound, ridiculed and abused and heard the rioting crowds screaming for his blood: "Crucify him! Crucify him!" Disregarding their own fear and repulsion for what was taking place, the women pushed their way into the jostling crowd to get close enough to comfort him by their presence. All the more because the other disciples had deserted him, these faithful ones wanted Jesus to know they were there. The women remained in the crowd as it surged through the city and outside the gate to Golgotha. There they witnessed his painful passion until mid-afternoon when "Jesus let out a loud cry and died" (Mk 15:37).

When Joseph of Arimathea took Jesus' body, wrapped it in fresh linen cloth and laid it in his own new tomb, the group of women who had come with him from Galilee followed be-

hind. They saw the tomb and the manner in which the body
was buried. They watched Joseph roll the huge stone across the
entrance and depart. But they remained until they were obliged
to leave and begin Sabbath preparations. Even then, Mary
Magdalene and the other Mary tarried, sitting there, facing the
tomb (cf. Mt 27:61).

It is important to pause and ponder the phrase just quoted,
for it is more than a simple description of the scene. The words
"sitting there, facing the tomb" are a clue to our understanding of the Gospel's core message about Jesus. Many times over
Jesus had openly repeated what he wanted his disciples to remember and to believe about him: that, in accordance with the
Scriptures, he was to go to Jerusalem where he would suffer
greatly and be put to death, and then he would rise again after
three days.

At times they made no response at all to these somber
predictions, as though they had not even heard them. When
they did hear them, it was without comprehension, and they
reacted with fear (Mk 9:32; Lk 9:45), with anger (Mt 16:22),
with sadness or grief (Mt 17:23). "Pay attention to what I am
telling you," he would admonish them (Lk 9:44), but still his
meaning eluded their understanding.

How, then, did they come at last to believe and to understand? And by what means are *we* able to open *our* minds and
hearts to his meaning for us today? The answers to these questions begin to emerge at the sealed burial chamber where those
first women disciples kept vigil in quiet contemplation.
Strangely, it was their pensive presence to the reality of that dark
hour which would prepare them inwardly for what they would

encounter at Sabbath's end. For upon their return on the third day, they were to find the tomb empty and his body nowhere in sight. Moreover, they were to receive an amazing message that would bathe their pain in light, transforming sorrow and fear into joy and courageous faith.

What was this profound transformation of faith that was to completely captivate them and, later, the other disciples to whom they would be sent to announce this good news? The letters of the apostle Paul, which precede the written Gospels, pinpoint the essence of Christian belief about Jesus as it was passed on to him by Peter and the others who knew and followed Jesus personally:

> I handed down to you as of primary importance what I, in turn, had received: namely that Christ died for our sins in accordance with the Scriptures; that he was buried; that he was raised on the third day in accordance with the Scriptures. (1 Cor 15:3, 4)

In other words: In fulfillment of the ancient Hebrew Scriptures, the redemptive power of Jesus was released in the world through his suffering, death and resurrection. This passion, death and resurrection of the Lord, the Paschal Mystery, is but *one reality* — and it is precisely the wholeness of this central truth about Jesus that gives meaning to the lives of all who would ever follow him. It is the oneness of this event that Paul had come to understand:

> My goal is to know [Christ] and the power of his resurrection, to understand the fellowship of his sufferings and become conformed to his death in the

hope of somehow attaining resurrection from the
dead. (Ph 3:10, 11)

Initially, Paul's personal experience was of the *risen* Jesus
— an encounter so powerful that it redirected the whole course
of his life. (This story is recounted three times in Acts 9:1-19;
22:1-21; 26:2-23.) His conversion came with dramatic swift-
ness, making him an immediate and steadfast believer in the
risen Jesus and a staunch defender of his New Way. But if Paul
was to be a true follower of this risen Jesus, he would have to
come to know the suffering and crucified Jesus as well. "This
man is a chosen instrument of mine," The Lord had said of Paul
in a vision to Ananias, "and I will show him how much he will
have to suffer for my name" (Acts 9:15, 16). As Paul's new way
of life unfolded before him, there were numerous occasions for
its full meaning to be learned from his own sufferings, trials and
daily dyings. It was in and through these circumstances that he
came to know the suffering Lord so intimately that he could
say, "I have been crucified with Christ! It is no longer I who
live; it is Christ who lives in me" (Gal 2:19-20).

Paul's letters leave no doubt that for him and for every
follower of Jesus, the transforming experience of the Risen Lord
is essentially linked with the drama of his passion and death.
This is the core memory that the believers of Jesus' own day
preserved and passed on in spoken word, just as it later became
the foundation for all of Paul's writings. By the end of the first
century, it was from this central event that the four evangelists
had created similar yet uniquely different Gospel portraits of
Jesus the Messiah, the Son of God.

And what of us? The faith of those first believers is the same faith that has been handed on to us and by which we are being saved at this very moment if we hold fast to it (cf. 1 Cor 15:2). Often in our lives we are as bewildered as they, particularly with regard to suffering and pain: we, too, react with fear, with anger, with sadness or grief. It is to illumine our own understanding that we pause here and enter into the darkness — but also into the light — of Christ's suffering and death on the cross. Only as we sit facing his tomb ourselves, do we begin to recognize that his passion is the goal and fulfillment of his life and teaching and that our redemption is achieved by death and resurrection together.

God calls all of us to live our own paschal mystery in union with Jesus. In the Synoptic Gospels (Mark, Matthew and Luke) Jesus follows the first prediction of his passion with this challenge:

> If you wish to come after me you must deny yourself, take up your cross, and follow me. For if you wish to save your life you will lose it, but if you are willing to lose your life for my sake and that of the Gospel you will save it. (cf. Mk 8:34, 35; Mt 16:24, 25; Lk 9:23, 24, adapted)

Today's world does not readily listen to the language of self-renunciation and willing embrace of suffering which this passage prescribes as the way to fullness of life. But Jesus does not soften his words for those who want to be his followers, for "I have come," he said, "that you might have life and have it abundantly" (Jn 10:10).

The two Marys finally left the tomb to prepare spices and perfumes with which to anoint the body of Jesus (Lk 23:56). After the Sabbath observance they would return to perform this burial service for him, without any hint of the amazing events to come or of the message that would forever change their lives. We shall return with them and the experience is likely to open our minds and hearts as well. Because we have watched reflectively here at the tomb of the dead Christ, we shall understand and rejoice anew in this fundamental truth of Christian faith: To follow Jesus is to share his life which is both *Amen* (so be it!) and *Alleluia* (praise God!) Not *Amen* alone. Not *Alleluia* alone. But *Amen!* and *Alleluia!* together. To believe and embrace this teaching is to find strength and perseverance for the *Amen* times as well as fulfillment and joy in the *Alleluia* times. It is to grow in our understanding of what it means to make the Gospel one's Way of Life.

For Your Meditation...

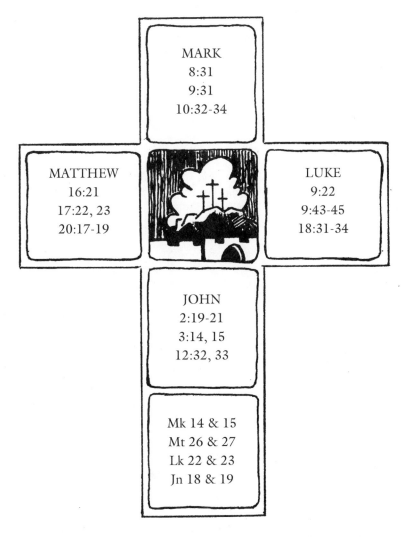

MARK
8:31
9:31
10:32-34

MATTHEW
16:21
17:22, 23
20:17-19

LUKE
9:22
9:43-45
18:31-34

JOHN
2:19-21
3:14, 15
12:32, 33

Mk 14 & 15
Mt 26 & 27
Lk 22 & 23
Jn 18 & 19

We proclaim Christ crucified... for God's foolishness is wiser
than human wisdom, and God's weakness is stronger than
human strength. (1 Cor 1:23, 25)

2

The Easter Message: "Go to Galilee"

Tell us, Mary, what did you see on the way? "I saw the tomb of the now living Christ. I saw the glory of Christ now risen. I saw angels who gave witness; the cloths, too, which once had covered his head and limbs. Christ my hope has arisen. He will go before his own into Galilee." (Sequence: Mass of Easter)

The Sabbath now over, we return with the women of Galilee to the burial site of Jesus. Once again we feel compelled to pause at this sacred place. Not in sadness as before, but this time in amazement and wonder at the now empty tomb where heavenly messengers appear and speak startling words to us.

All four Gospels recount this most glorious moment in human history, each offering its own piece to our understanding of the Easter message. We also begin to recognize in these narratives that the Gospels are unique documents, essentially similar for their carefully preserved faith traditions, yet distinctly different by reason of each evangelist's intuitive style, focus and historic setting. These similarities and differences are readily apparent in the Synoptic Gospels of Mark, Matthew and Luke.

John, on the other hand, is so characteristically different from the others as to warrant separate treatment.

Keep in mind that not only the Gospels but all of Scripture has come to us through the ponderings, creativity and purposes of human authors. God spoke to their hearts and they responded by shaping oral traditions of faith into God's Word preserved in writing. Their intention was to instruct, guide and encourage believers of their own day by reminding them of God's presence in their past and ongoing history. In the Divine Author's plan, however, their inspired documents would proclaim God's love for all peoples of every age.

The Empty-Tomb Accounts and the Easter Message

(Note: Beginning with the Synoptics, our reading order follows the probable dating of each Gospel: Mark (AD 70), Matthew (AD 80-85), and Luke (AD 80-90). The Scripture references are given with the recommendation that each account be read in the Bible before proceeding to the following reflections.)

Mark's Account: (Read Mk 16:1-8)

In Mark's Gospel, we approach the tomb together with Mary Magdalene and Mary the mother of James and Salome. As we hurry along, we remember a detail we hadn't thought of until this moment. The stone! With our own eyes we had seen the man from Arimathea roll it across the entrance. It was huge. Not even our combined strength will be able to budge it. Looking from one to the other, we voice our predicament in unison: "Who will roll back the stone for us?" Turning straight ahead to the entrance we can see that the stone is already rolled back. It glistens in the early morning sun which casts a shaft of light along the ground toward the opening, as if to invite our entrance. Once inside, we are startled by the presence of a young man clothed in white and seated to the right of the bench where Jesus' body had been left for the completion of the burial wrapping. To our amazement, he speaks: "Do not be alarmed! You are looking for Jesus of Nazareth who was crucified. He has risen; he is not here. Behold the place where they laid him. But go and tell his disciples and Peter, *he is going ahead of you to Galilee*; there you will see him as he told you." Now ponder God's word in the quiet of your heart. Listen closely and hear Jesus' personal message for you:

THE EASTER MESSAGE IN MARK

I have travelled this way before you that you may learn to look for me in the Galilee of your own life. That is where I am. *Come, follow me there*, for my life continues now in your life.

Matthew's Account: (Read Mt 28:1-10)

This time we join the two Marys who had stayed long after everyone else had withdrawn from the tomb and who are now returning to the site. Just as we reach the tomb, we hear the rumbling noise of an earthquake and the ground underfoot begins to tremble. At the same time, an angel of the Lord

appears suddenly from the heavens. Looking like a flash of light-
ning in garments white as snow, this apparition easily rolls back
the huge stone and takes its place on top of it! The guards sta-
tioned here by Pilate are paralyzed with fear. We are in some-
what the same condition — but the angel looks at us and says:
"Do not be afraid! I know that you are looking for Jesus who
was crucified. He is not here, for he has risen just as he said.
Come and see the place where he lay. Then go quickly and tell
his disciples, 'He has been raised from the dead, and he is going ahead of you to Galilee; there you will see him. Behold I
have told you.'"

With a strange mixture of joy and fear in our hearts, we
make haste to announce the news to the others. As we go along,
Jesus himself comes to meet us on the road! Yes, we are sure it
is he — the familiar countenance and walk, the warm smile and
compassionate gaze, the loving greeting of peace. How good
it is to hear his voice! "Do not be afraid. Go tell my brothers
to *go to Galilee*, and there they will see me." Now ponder God's
word in the quiet of your heart. Listen closely and hear Jesus'
personal message for you:

THE EASTER MESSAGE IN MATTHEW

Go to Galilee: Embrace your life as I did mine; embrace the wholeness of your own passion, death and
resurrection. This has been my life for you and it is
your life in me until I come again. Do not be afraid
for I am present in all that happens to you.

Luke's Account: (Read Lk 24:1-11)

We go now with Mary Magdalene, Joanna, Mary the mother of James and a number of other women from Galilee to take spices and perfumed oils to the tomb. We see that the stone has been rolled back and the tomb is open. But upon entering, it is immediately apparent to us that the body of Jesus is not there. As we look at one another in total bewilderment, we are suddenly aware of the two men standing there in dazzling garments. Our knees give out and we sink to the ground trembling. The men speak: "Why are you looking for the living among the dead? He is not here; he has risen. *Remember what he said* to you while he will still in Galilee: that the Son of Man would have to be handed over to sinners and be crucified, and rise on the third day." Yes, we can recall many occasions when he spoke these very words — but we never understood what he was trying to teach us. We leave the tomb quietly, thinking back and pondering within ourselves all that has taken place. By the time we reach the place where the eleven have been staying, we are filled with excitement about our visit to the tomb. But when we try to share the experience with the apostles, they call it "nonsense" and refuse to believe any of it. Now ponder God's word in the quiet of your heart. Listen closely and hear Jesus' personal message for you:

THE EASTER MESSAGE IN LUKE

Remember! It will not always be easy. You will have
some happiness, some success, some satisfaction and
joy in your life. But what will really enable you to
grasp the meaning of it all are those things that will
be difficult to bear: trials, disappointments, failures,
illness, separation, death. But *remember*: This is my
Galilee. It is a beautiful land, my Galilee. And *remember*: I died on a cross so that you, too, could pass
through your Galilee on your way to Jerusalem and
home.

Several points are fittingly made here. The first is that our
intuitive reading of the Synoptic tomb scenes allows us to by-
pass the perplexing lesser details (e.g. Was the stone still in place
or not?) and focus on the more subtle nuances of meaning. It
is from these underlying differences that the message emerges
in stages. And as the message unfolds, the person of Jesus continues to be revealed to us in stages as well. Mark's empty-tomb
message reveals a Jesus who has made the journey before us that
we may know and follow his way. Matthew's Jesus commissions
us to go forth on that journey, promising to walk along with
us lest we lose the way. Luke's Jesus reminds us that it is his
road we travel, that we must pass through suffering and death
on our way to resurrection and the fullness of life. If we were
to associate just one word with each Synoptic's Easter message
(a useful study help), our list would read as follows:

Mark	COME!
Matthew	GO!
Luke	REMEMBER!

As for the striking similarities in the three traditions, we need to pay attention to them. Where more than one Gospel contains substantially the same material, we have a clue that the story is rooted in the earliest oral proclamations. The evangelists take care to preserve the living faith passed on to their communities by the original eye witnesses and ministers of the Word (Lk 1:1-4).

Finally, it is from the reference to Galilee in each of the Synoptic accounts that a spiritual geography of the Gospels begins to emerge. Mark and Matthew clearly designate Galilee as the place where the risen Lord is to be encountered. Luke recalls Galilee as the familiar place where we have already seen the Lord and points to our need to remember those privileged encounters. What, then, is the significance of Galilee in regard to the Easter message?

Galilee, we know, is the place where Jesus spent most of his life on earth. It is where he grew up, received an education, learned a trade. It is where he left home and went out on his own and developed friendships with men and women who came into his life. Galilee is where Jesus lived and taught and healed — where he had happy days with little children and frustrating days with people who misunderstood him or who just refused to listen to him. Galilee is the place where Jesus grew in an understanding of the meaning of his life and where he set about to accomplish the Father's will for him one day at a time. His life in Galilee was busy and full and demanding — and often disappointing.

Now from the empty tomb we hear the land of Galilee specified as a spiritual reality, our meeting place with the

Crucified and Risen Lord. Galilee, then, symbolizes life: Jesus' life and our life. It is the life that Jesus lived as an example and as an encouragement for us (Mark); the life that he urges us to embrace completely and wholeheartedly (Matthew); the life that he reminds us is lived in joy and in sorrow, and always in relation to God (Luke). While each account enriches the others with its own emphasis, the Easter message in all three Gospels is the same. We are invited, challenged and reminded simply to *Go to Galilee* — to participate in the oneness of Jesus' passion, death and resurrection in our own lives.

❦

John's Account (Read Jn 20)

Characteristically, the Gospel of John (AD 90-100) makes its own contribution to the Easter message in a manner quite different from the Synoptic accounts. Here, Mary Magdalene finds the stone rolled back, assumes the body has been stolen and immediately runs to make that report to Peter and "the other disciple whom Jesus loved." The two disciples come and enter the tomb, observe the burial cloths that had covered the body, then return home, "for they did not yet understand the Scripture that he had to rise from the dead." Remaining outside the tomb, Mary peers in and sees two angels who ask why she is crying but who do not speak the Easter message. Turning, she sees another figure who she presumes to be the gardener. Only when he speaks her name does she recognize Jesus who commissions her to spread the news that he is alive and is "ascending to my Father and your Father, to my God and your God." Mary hastens to tell the disciples all Jesus had said, concluding her story with this profession of faith: "I have seen the Lord!"

This is the first of three resurrection appearances of Jesus in John 20. On the evening of that same day, Jesus appeared to the disciples and showed them his hands and his side. They rejoiced at his presence and eagerly reported to Thomas who had not been with them, "We have seen the Lord!" As with Mary Magdalene, they now understood the Scripture about his rising from the dead and acknowledged this belief in their profession of faith. Thomas, however, who had not witnessed the sight of Jesus' wounded hands and feet, was unable to believe. One week later, Jesus came again when all the disciples, including Thomas, were together. After greeting them all with peace, he spoke directly to Thomas: "Bring your finger here and look at my hands, and bring your hand and put it into my side, and be not unbelieving, but believe." Thomas answered Jesus with his own profound profession of faith: "My Lord and my God!"

In John, then, the message from the empty tomb comes not from heavenly beings nor even from the Risen Jesus. It comes, rather, from Mary Magdalene on the first Easter morning, from the disciples assembled that same evening and from Thomas one week later. It emerges as they come to understand the oneness of Jesus' suffering, death and resurrection and profess their belief in this truth. At the conclusion of these three episodes, Jesus turns to us and asks *our* profession of faith with these words: "Blessed are you who have not seen and have believed."

We may now complete our study-help list of one-word associations with each evangelist's Easter message:

Mark	COME!
Matthew	GO!
Luke	REMEMBER!
John	BELIEVE!

In effect, John is saying: Believe in Mark's invitation to follow Jesus; believe in Matthew's sending you forth in company with Jesus; believe in Luke's admonition to recall what Jesus has said and done in your life; most of all, believe "that you may have life in his name."

We may wonder about the symbolism of Galilee in John's unfolding of the Easter message. Unlike the Synoptic traditions, no mention is made of it here. For our purposes right now, that treatment is deferred to Chapter Nine where we will encounter the Risen Lord on the shore of Galilee's lake in John 21. This charming epilogue to the fourth Gospel is a vivid show-and-tell experience of what followers of Jesus can expect as they embrace his life in their own. Here Jesus gives a final teaching to the Eleven and to us on just what it means to *Go to Galilee.*

For Your Meditation...

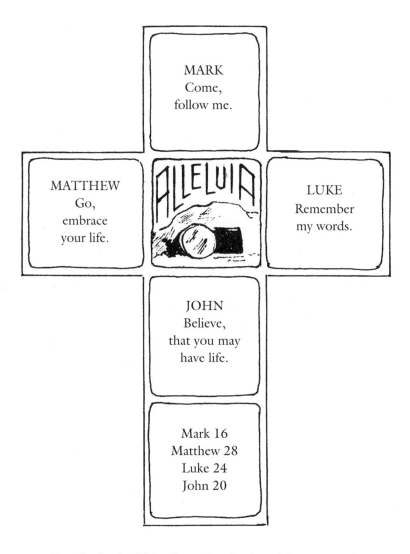

MARK
Come,
follow me.

MATTHEW
Go,
embrace
your life.

ALLELUIA

LUKE
Remember
my words.

JOHN
Believe,
that you may
have life.

Mark 16
Matthew 28
Luke 24
John 20

But God raised him from the dead, and he appeared over many days to those who had gone up with him from Galilee to Jerusalem. (Acts 13:30-31)

Part Two

The Spiritual Geography
of the Gospels

3

Reading the Land

Five gospels record the life of Jesus. Four you will find
in books, and one you will find in the land they call
holy. Read the fifth gospel and the world of the four
will open to you.[1]

Becoming familiar with the land that produced the Bible
is a fascinating way to enhance one's understanding of Sacred
Scripture. Much as reading the stage setting puts the plot and
characters of a play in perspective, so "reading the land" provides a vivid backdrop for the Bible's unfolding story. More
accurately, as we shall see, the land itself tells the story through
the symbolism of its geography.

Geography studies the regions of the earth in terms of
natural conditions and resources: land, elevation, water, air,
climate, animal and plant life. Its purpose is to provide practi-
cal knowledge of the physical elements of earth toward an understanding of their effect on this planet's inhabitants.

---

[1] The concept of the land as "the fifth gospel" is attributed to the French philologist
and historian, Joseph Ernest Renan (1823-1892).

As with all other branches of human knowledge, geography has its origins in the common wisdom of primitive civilizations. People learned early on that environment has significant consequences for the fact and quality of their existence and for any endeavors they might pursue. Then, as now, they learned more slowly that personal response to one's surroundings is more important still.

But the earthly setting in which we humans fashion our patterns of life and work is more than the subject of a fascinating natural science. The world we live in is a magnificent theophany — a visible manifestation of the invisible God:

> From the creation of the world, God's invisible attributes of eternal power and divinity have been accessible to human knowledge through what can be perceived (Rm 1:20).

More wondrous still is the realization that the world we inhabit is our meeting place with God — for it is in and through this world that God chooses to communicate with us.

In the plan of God, a small piece of land in the Middle East is center stage for this divine-human drama of salvation history. Characteristically, God's predesigned choice of this place is ingenious, for more than being simply the setting of our story it is, in its geography, the symbol of the drama itself. Tourist literature describes the Holy Land as "a sampler of startling contrasts within a surprisingly small frame." Sojourners in Israel soon discover the aptness of this description as they experience dramatic changes in the physical features of the land within very short distances.

Five main features of the Holy Land symbolize the stages of our spiritual journey. The characteristic qualities of these terrains, which are already part of our human experience, typify how the land speaks to the meaning of life:

1. The Sea and the Fertile Plains — Water, which is essential to all earthly life and growth, can be refreshing, cooling, cleansing, calm and restful. But it can change quickly, becoming rough and stormy, frightening and life threatening. In the Gospels, the lake and the land around it is the terrain of everyday events and daily occupations with all their ups and downs. Here is where we interact with family, friends, co-workers and strangers in the ordinary times and, yes, the humdrum times of life. Most often in the Gospels this is the setting for God's call and our response, for lessons to be learned, for dreams to be dreamed, and for miracles and healings to take place. It is also here that we discover the inner strength of God's presence in life's unexpected turbulences.

2. The Mountains — This terrain is rugged, uneven and all uphill. There is danger of falling, of being wounded, bruised, broken. From below, the climb may seem too arduous to attempt, too impossible to achieve. It is not unusual, however, that with perseverance (and oftentimes the encouragement and help of others), we are surprised with the accomplishment of our goals and dreams. Reaching the top we are rewarded with a breathtaking, God's-eye view of our situation. The Gospels teach us that life's mountain experiences are encounters with God which provide us with moments of clarity and of connectedness. On the mountain we may receive new insights of faith;

we may be graced with power to overcome temptation or sin; most surely we are strengthened for the continuing journey.

3. The Road — It is the road we travel that gives direction to our journey. It unfolds before us along ways that can be straight or winding, uphill and down, over and through the varied terrains of life. Often we come to a fork in the road which means we are faced with choices and decisions. We meet with detours along the way which offer no choice at all but to follow the only route open at the time. Looking back, we know where the road has taken us thus far. We know, too, that we have made mistakes along the way, perhaps some major ones that seemingly have changed our course. We may have to repair old bridges or build new ones for the road to continue. But all that has happened is essential to our story and in looking back we recognize God's presence throughout. While our vision of the road ahead is limited and unclear, we continue with hearts assured that God will remain with us to the end.

4. The Desert — While most of us would not choose the desert experiences of life, every one of us must sojourn through this wilderness on our way to the Promised Land. The desert is austere and desolate and can be uncomfortable, lonely and depressing. Because it is so difficult to travel here, one must leave behind much of what has seemed important and vital. In contrast, however, the desert can provide a haven, a place apart, a retreat encounter with God. At its proper time, in fact, the wilderness can come alive with exquisite plants and flowers. The desert, therefore, is most often a time of struggle, of purification, of confrontation with self — all demanding honesty, patience and waiting. But it may also be the time of call and preparation, a time of purest joy because the emptied self has made room for God's bountiful love to enter in.

5. Jerusalem and the Temple — In our journey through these varied terrains, we are always on the road that leads to Jerusalem. The city is holy because of the Temple which is the house of God. And because the Temple is the place of God's presence, it is also a house of prayer for all the people. The symbolism is powerful for Christian spirituality which teaches that we ourselves are now the Temple of the Living Spirit of God. We journey with our God — not alone, but as the community of God's People. God is present in all the happenings of our lives and this we remember and celebrate when we gather together in prayer and rituals of worship. Jerusalem with its Temple further symbolizes our ultimate destiny. For one day we shall leave behind the fertile plains, rugged mountains and parched deserts, as the road makes its final ascent to the heavenly Jerusalem, our home. In this new Jerusalem there will be no Temple because the Lord God and the Lamb will be its Temple. Symbolism gives way to reality and we shall dwell with God forever in the Everlasting City.

These five geographic settings of the Gospels function prominently in the portrayal of Jesus and his earthly mission. The evangelists make skillful use of natural surroundings and particular locations to shed light on the theological significance of Jesus and his teaching. In like manner, the geography of the Gospels sheds light on the Christian's spiritual journey. Life, for the most part, is ordinary — or so it seems. But the pilgrim who moves through life as he or she finds it, granting each terrain its importance in the unfolding story, is graced with moments of seeing beyond the ordinary.

While all four canonical Gospels take us through the whole of the land, each evangelist seems to focus on a particular feature as a place of importance for Jesus. In each place we come to know another facet of Jesus' personality. And as we travel the spiritual geography of the Gospels, the meaning of the Easter message, "Go to Galilee," emerges in sharper relief.

Let us now open that fifth gospel — the land — and journey through its spiritual geography as a profoundly simple way of seeing and hearing what the written Gospels have to say. To read the fifth gospel is to allow the imagery of the land to speak to one's heart, for the heart's inner vision sees into realities beyond what the mind alone observes. But the mind responds to the stirrings of the heart with its own unique gift of contemplation. The mind studies and ponders and comes to rest prayerfully in God's Word alive in the heart. Truly, the land makes the difference and through it the reader discovers an engaging way to deepen enjoyment and comprehension of the entire Bible.

> Five gospels record the life of Jesus. Four you will find in books, and one you will find in the land they call holy. Read the fifth gospel and the world of the four will open to you.

4

By the Sea with Mark

Such a large crowd gathered around him that he got into a boat on the sea and sat down, while the whole crowd gathered along the sea on the land. (Mk 4:1)

The land circling the Sea of Galilee (which is in reality a freshwater lake) stretches beyond surrounding slopes to farmlands and palm groves, fruit orchards and cotton fields, to hills, mountains and valleys. This landscape is delightful to behold at any season, but in springtime it is rainbow colored with wild flowers in great abundance and variety. The stony areas of white limestone and black basalt create interesting patterns of contrast.

The lake itself is a captivating sight. "God has created the seven seas but the Sea of Galilee is His special delight," wrote ancient Jewish sages. Situated in the deepest valley on earth (part of the Syrian-African Rift), the heart-shaped Sea of Galilee is almost seven hundred feet below sea level. It is thirteen miles long and eight at its widest expanse. Its shimmering blue water is clear and changes to a deep sapphire tone at the end of day.

From the Gospels and other early writings, we know that the land of Galilee in Jesus' day was no less arrayed with natural splendor and rich productivity (Mk 2:23; Mt 6:28, 29). We know, too, that the public ministry of Jesus was centered around the lake. After his expulsion from the synagogue in Nazareth, Jesus adopted Capernaum, twenty-five miles away on the northwestern shore of the Sea of Galilee, as his own town (Mk 2:1; Mt 4:13). Like the other settlements around the lake, Capernaum's chief industry was fishing but, because of its particular location on the lake, it had added significance as a city.

First of all, it was a border city between Galilee and Gaulanitis, territories ruled respectively by Herod Antipas and Philip, sons of Herod the Great. The major trade route from Damascus to Egypt, the Via Maris, passed through Capernaum. In addition, it was a port of entry for caravans from the East carrying their rich wares to Mediterranean seaports for shipment to markets in the rest of the known world. All of this trafficking necessitated border checkpoints and a customs bureau for the collection of taxes on merchandise passing from one region to another. Finally, there was a military presence in Capernaum — divisions of the Roman Legion assigned to guard the road built along the city's edge. Being part of a mainstream Roman province with a cosmopolitan flavor had its advantages and challenges for Jesus' ministry. Gospel retrospect and our own reflection give us a sense that he also enjoyed his home and his life around the lake.

As the Gospel written closest to the time of Jesus, Mark reflects the spontaneity and enthusiasm of a storyteller bursting to share the story with others. There is an aura of mystery and even secrecy about Mark's Jesus and yet the same Jesus is down to earth and approachable. He has a sense of urgency about his mission that keeps him on the move all over Galilee: "Let us go elsewhere, to the neighboring country towns so that I may proclaim the good news there also. That is what I have come to do" (1:38).

He preaches in the synagogue and teaches in the fields and from a fishing boat anchored just offshore. He listens with interest and compassion to what people think and feel. By his own example, he shows them how to encourage, admonish and forgive one another in love. And so he makes his way along the lake, choosing those he wants to share his ministry — to whom he will later entrust it (1:16-20; 2:14; 3:13-19).

It is our story that is being told on and around the lake. This is the ordinary terrain of our lives where Jesus is present and interacting with us in the situations and experiences of day-to-day living. Extraordinary things do happen here. Jesus works mighty deeds and miracles in our lives: he heals our ills (6:55,56), quiets our storms (4:35-41), renews our life (5:21-43), satisfies our physical and spiritual hunger (6:34-44; 8:1-9), comes to us and calms our fears (6:45-52). But these encounters often occur in such ordinary ways that we do not always recognize him in our midst. If our focus is mainly on the miraculous aspect of what Jesus does, we can miss the sound of his voice, the gentleness of his touch. We can fail to understand the signs of his presence because we have not yet grasped his preference for simple, human ways of communicating: a word spoken, some bread broken.

"Secrecy" about Jesus is a prominent characteristic of

Mark's Gospel which opens with a simple statement of Jesus'
divine origin: "The beginning of the good news of Jesus Christ,
the Son of God" (1:1). Then follows the baptism of Jesus in
the Jordan River when the Spirit descends upon him and a voice
from heaven affirms: "You are my beloved Son; in you I am
well pleased" (1:10, 11). Yet the remainder of the Gospel por-
trays Jesus as keeping his identity carefully hidden (7:36; 9:9).
Scripture scholars refer to this as the Messianic Secret — the
refusal of Jesus to accept the title of Messiah until the hour when
he would show by his death and resurrection what it really
meant. Peter had once proclaimed, "You are the Messiah!" —
but was sternly reprimanded for his objection to Jesus' terms
for Messiahship: that he "had to suffer greatly, be rejected by
the elders, the chief priests and the scribes, be put to death and
rise after three days" (8:31).

Here by the water — an element essential to all life and
the symbol of our baptism — Jesus teaches the meaning of his
life and ours. Yes, he is the Messiah, the Anointed One of God,
the deliverer of his people. But he is the Suffering Messiah foretold by the prophets and come to deliver us from the slavery of
sin by dying and rising to new life. Anyone wishing to be his
disciple can do so only by sharing in his sufferings, by taking
up his or her own cross and following in his footsteps (8:27-
38). With the death of Jesus on the cross, what had been hushed
throughout the Gospel is proclaimed openly; what had not been
understood by Jesus' closest followers is voiced aloud by an
unbelieving centurion: "Truly, this man was the Son of God"
(15:39).

The characteristically serene surface of the Sea of Galilee

can be churned into a violent storm on short notice. Similarly, our lives can be altered just as quickly as the lake changes in a sudden squall. In some of life's storms, Jesus seems to be unconcerned about our problems, unaware of our desperation. Worried about our very survival, we awaken him with our frantic prayer. When the time is right, he speaks to the sea and the wind, and everything grows calm. He speaks to us: "Why are you so afraid? Do you not yet have faith?" (4:35-41).

There are times when he comes walking to us on the water as we try to row our boat with the wind against us. "Take courage! It is I. Do not be afraid!" He gets into the boat with us and the wind dies down (6:45-51). We are taken aback by such happenings, yet our minds remain closed to the meaning of these events. But as we ponder the rough experiences of life we begin to wonder, "Who can this be that the wind and the sea obey him?" Gradually, we come to recognize that God visits us in many ways: in illness and in health, in failure and in success, in sorrow and in joy, in old age as well as in youth. In our wavering moments, we hear the voice of Jesus saying, "Fear is useless. What is needed is trust."

Freedom from fear is a gift which, when accepted, seems to call forth yet another — a deepened sense of the presence of Jesus in all the details of our story. And so we see him walking along the shore (2:13) and we quicken our steps to join him there. He stays close to the lake where the crowds gather round him (5:21), so we sit down at the water's edge and listen to his stories. We grow weary and he invites us to "Come away privately, just yourselves, to a desert place and rest a bit." So we climb into the boat and go off with him to a deserted place

(6:31, 32). After a time, we are no longer surprised to find him close by — for we have learned to look for him in the ordinary happenings of life as well as in times of our most desperate need.

Reading Mark's Gospel means returning often to the lake and its shores, to our first encounters with Jesus. Here we can feel his gaze fixed on us and hear his call, "Come after me" (1:17; cf. 2:14) — an invitation he extends many times over in the course of our lives. We must return, as well, to Mark's message from the empty tomb where the "Follow me" of Jesus is echoed once more: "I have gone before you to Galilee. Galilee is where you will see me. I am alive and my life continues in your life." This is the reason for our Christian faith and hope as we travel with him in footprints he has already marked out for us in life's varied terrains.

For Your Meditation…

LORD, I AM HERE

Lord, I am here — But, child, I look for thee
    elsewhere and nearer me.
Lord, that way moans a wide insatiate sea:
    how can I come to Thee? —
Set foot upon the water, test and see
    if thou canst come to Me. —
Couldst Thou not send a boat to carry me,
    or a dolphin swimming free? —
Nay, boat nor fish if thy will faileth thee:
    For My will too is free —
O Lord, I am afraid. — Take hold of Me;
    I am stronger than the sea. —
Save, Lord, I perish! — I have hold of thee,
    I made and rule the sea. —
I bring thee to the haven where thou wouldst be.

Christina G. Rossetti (1830-1894)

Through the sea was your path;
    your way, through the mighty waters,
    though your footsteps were unseen.
    (Psalm 77:20)

5

Climbing Matthew's Mountains

When he saw the crowds, he went up the mountain.
After he sat down, his disciples came to him. (Mt 5:1,2)

The country of Israel is formed by three north-to-south
parallel land strips of different geographical character. A coastal
plain running along its western boundary at the Mediterranean
Sea is home for more than half of the country's population. The
eastern strip is the Rift Valley which contains, besides the Sea
of Galilee and the Jordan River, the Dead Sea which, at thirteen
hundred feet below sea level, is the lowest place on earth. The
central strip of the land is formed by mountains that rise from
the coastal plain and descend sharply into the Jordan Valley.

The northern region of Galilee has mountain elevations
from eighteen hundred to four thousand feet which rise above
rounded land masses and rolling hills. At the foot of Mount
Carmel these are interrupted by the fertile Valley of Esdraelon
reaching inland from the coastal plain. But the mountains rise
again, stretching into Samaria and through the southern arid
regions which comprise more than half of the country's total

land area. Here they become the harsh and barren Judean Wilderness — the haunt of "serpents and scorpions" mentioned in Dt 8:15. From Judea through the Negev to the southern boundary at the Red Sea, the range takes on multiple formations, colors and textures caused by millennia of wind erosion and by flood waters of the rainy seasons.

It is against this varied mountain terrain that Matthew's portrait of Jesus and the thrust of his mission emerge. Writing ten to fifteen years after Mark and some fifty years after the death of Jesus, Matthew sensed a need within the early Church for an organized presentation of their faith beliefs. Moreover, his own Jewish-Christian community had a particular need for some kind of continuity with their past as well as guidelines for approaching an unknown future. Their Temple had been destroyed, they were no longer welcome in the synagogues and with increasing numbers of Gentiles coming into the fold, these Jewish converts were quickly becoming a marginalized group. All of this, coupled with continuing political unrest and persecution in the land, was cause enough for the climate of tension and anxiety in which they tried to follow Jesus of Galilee. Where were they headed? What were they to teach their children? And how could they prepare them for responsible adulthood in this confused world?

Twenty centuries later, we can relate to similar kinds of situations in our Church and world — and the questions are ours, no adaptation needed. Along with the early Christians, we discover that following the Lord sometimes means climbing with him to a higher terrain for a clearer view of life. So we make our way up the mountainside and gather around Jesus who begins to teach us. He speaks from his heart and we hear his words from within the depths of our own hearts:

> More than anything, I want for you what you yearn for yourselves — a happy life. Because you believe in me, you shall be happy — for happiness is rooted in your faith. But faith must be animated by love that is willing to work to spread the reign of God throughout the world.
>
> The world's misery stems from its pursuit of material wealth, power and selfish ambition. Such gains of fleeting satisfaction are always at the expense of the human rights and dignity of God's anawim, the little people.
>
> Happiness, rather, belongs to you who are poor in spirit and who seek after holiness — for you are already in the reign of God on earth. And as you embrace poverty, sorrow and persecution as part of your life, you will become more merciful and compassionate peacemakers. Your reward is great in heaven, for God's reign will reach fulfillment in you. So be glad and rejoice, you whose hearts are set on God! You are in the spirit and mode of the prophets of old who accomplished great wonders in the same way. (Sermon on the Mount Mt 5:1-12 Adapted)

In these beatitudes or blessings of happiness, Jesus manifests a compassionate awareness of the struggle good people are up against. And in keeping with the evangelist's purpose, Matthew's Jesus is already hinting at his post-resurrection message to the women making their way from the empty tomb: "Go to Galilee — embrace your life as I did mine." Not without help, however. From his own and other traditions, Matthew fashions a collection of the Master's teachings into one

long Sermon on the Mount (Chapters 5-7) in which Jesus offers instructions and encouragement for Christian living, especially in times of trial and stress.

Matthew's portrait, then, is of Jesus the teacher, the new
Moses. Just as Moses taught the people the Law he had received
from God on Mount Horeb (Ex 19, 20), so does Jesus ascend
a mountain to teach the fulfillment of that Law: how to live,
how to pray, how to be happy. "Do not think that I have come
to overturn the law or the prophets. I have come not to destroy but to fulfill" (5:17).

> Jesus took Peter and James and his brother John
> along and led them up a high mountain by them-
> selves. And he was transformed before them; his face
> shone like the sun while his clothing became as white
> as light (17:1, 2).

Perhaps more often than we realize, Jesus invites us to
climb to the very top of a mountain where the air is purer still
and where our inner vision is graced with deeper perceptions
of truth. Here we see Jesus, not merely in a new light, but Himself the light that illumines the path of our journey. In his
transfiguration he is joined by Moses and Elijah who converse
with him. For us it is a moment of transformation that puts us
in touch with our roots, our history and our God: "This is my
beloved Son, with whom I am well pleased; hear him." We hear
his voice and feel his presence and we are not afraid to descend
from the mountain — for Jesus, God-With-Us, remains with
us as we continue our journey (cf. Mt 17:1-8).

The Sermon on the Mount and the Transfiguration are remembered in two of the most beautiful places in the Holy Land. The Mount of Beatitudes is high above the Sea of Galilee, a blue jewel below. At this elevation there is a constant gentle breeze that carries aloft the sound of the lake's lapping waters. Mount Tabor, not far from Nazareth, is where the Transfiguration is commemorated. Standing alone in the Plain of Esdraelon, this mountain reaches its summit at just under two thousand feet from where a sweeping view of the beautiful fertile plain below may be seen for miles around.

But our mountain experiences are not always in pleasant settings nor do they always evoke the kind of reaction we share with Peter on Tabor: "Lord, it is good for us to be here!" The changing terrain can become harsh and desolate like the somber hills and stark cliffs of Judea where tradition places the site of Jesus' struggle against Satan. "The devil then took him up a very high mountain..." Times of loneliness and temptation are part of our human story and can be occasions of self-knowledge and of spiritual growth. A striking lesson to learn from the temptations of Jesus on this mountain is the power of a spirituality formed from God's Word alive in one's heart. With this strength, Jesus rid himself of the devil and "angels came and ministered to him" (cf. Mt 4:1-11).

From these few examples, we can draw some helpful conclusions about the mountainous terrains of life. First, we climb in various modes: sometimes as part of a large group, sometimes together with a few close companions — and at other times, by ourselves. In no instance, pleasant or painful, are we ever alone. "God is with us" is a predominant theme in Matthew, from his opening definition of the prophetic name, Emmanuel (1:23), to the final farewell of Jesus: "...I will be with you all the days until the end of the age" (28:20).

Secondly, what happens to us on the mountain is never for ourselves only. It was after his mountain temptations that Jesus began his public ministry. As the author of Hebrews notes in 2:18, "Since he himself was tested through what he suffered, he is able to help those who are tempted." We are told that when Jesus came down from the Mount of Beatitude, great crowds followed him and he went about attending to their physical and spiritual needs. Again, after his transfiguration on Tabor, Jesus and the three apostles came down from the mountain, approached the waiting crowds and immediately began to minister to them. Lastly, we cannot mistake the meaning of Jesus' commissioning ceremony for his disciples on the Mount of the Ascension in Galilee:

> The eleven disciples went into Galilee, to the mountain to which Jesus had directed them.... Jesus came and spoke to them, saying: "...go, therefore, and make disciples of all nations, baptizing them in the name of the Father, and of the Son, and of the Holy Spirit. Teach them to observe all that I have commanded you" (Mt 28:16-20).

It is clear that what we have received, we are to share in ministry to our families, our church, our world. Spreading the reign of God on earth can mean leading others to the foot of their mountain, or accompanying them on their ascent. When the climb is particularly steep or frightening, it may mean holding on to them or reaching out a hand to pull them over the top.

In his "studio" by the sea, Mark paints a portrait of the
Jesus of our daily encounters. On the mountain places where
Matthew prefers to paint, our meetings with Jesus may be less
frequent than those by the sea. But they are unforgettable occasions, treasured experiences that transform all the days and
years to come. The rugged mountain terrains of life provide us
with strength and perseverance for the road ahead.

For Your Meditation...

PSALM 121

I raise my eyes toward the mountains.
From where will my help come?
My help comes from the LORD,
the maker of heaven and earth.
God will not allow your foot to slip;
your guardian does not sleep.
Truly, the guardian of Israel
never slumbers nor sleeps.
The LORD is your guardian;
the LORD is your shade at your right hand.
By day the sun cannot harm you,
nor the moon by night.
The LORD will guard you from all evil,
will always guard your coming and going
both now and forever.

**Go outside and stand on the mountain before the LORD;
the LORD will be passing by.
(1 Kings 19:11)**

6

On the Road with Luke

Were not our hearts burning within us while he spoke
to us on the road, as he opened the Scriptures to us?
(Lk 24:32)

The Promised Land of the Hebrew Scriptures — Palestine of New Testament times — is today modern Israel.
Theodor Herzl, the Austrian Jew who inspired the founding
of the Jewish state in 1948, had a descriptive name for this tiny
land of contrasts. He called it *Altneuland*: Old-New Land.

The New Land is proud of such cities as Tel Aviv, the in-
dustrial, commercial and cultural center of Israel as well as its
entertainment capital; Haifa, the country's largest seaport and
trade center; Eilat where tourists enjoy fine hotels and beaches,
water sports and underwater nature reserves; and Jerusalem, the
capital and seat of government, expanded beyond the Old City
walls to become Israel's largest city. Many present-day urban
centers are built on or near biblical sites of the Old Land.

Approximately ninety per cent of Israel's more than five
million people are city dwellers. The remainder of the popula-

tion live varying lifestyles in small villages, housing developments or one of two types of cooperative communities, the kibbutz and the moshav. Nomadic tent-dwellers still move about the land with their flocks and meager possessions as in the days of Abraham. Ruins of early civilizations are to be found everywhere — in religious shrines and museums, under public buildings and private homes, in archaeological digs and restorations. The past seems as alive as the present along any road one might take, whether by the sea, up a mountain or down into a canyon, through the fields or across a desert wilderness. While we remain aware of the changing terrain, what captures our reflective consciousness is the continuity and importance of the journey.

Lucan emphasis shifts from the topography of the land to the journey through the land, symbolized by the road stretching ahead to the fulfillment of Jesus' mission and ours. So much is this the thrust of his message that Luke is the only evangelist to write a second volume to his Gospel, the Acts of the Apostles, in which he recounts the ongoing Christian journey and missionary activity after the Lord's ascension. Besides giving us a sense of continuity with the early Church, Acts provides us with hope and help for issues and difficulties facing the Church today. These are very real people we meet in Acts whose faith matured as they struggled with their own conflicting personalities and opinions while evolving from a sect within Judaism to a universal Church. Different matters and anxieties beset us today. But Scripture remains our story and the same Spirit who guided the early Church continues working in us.

Luke-Acts (the two-volume work is considered as a whole) furnishes us with a new portrait of Jesus and of our lives as his followers. An early legend claims the author of the third Gospel was also a fine artist, and attributes to him a portrait of Mary with the Christ Child: "Salus Populi Romani." (In subsequent centuries, artists were fond of making "Luke Painting the Blessed Virgin" the subject of their own paintings.) Luke's painted portrait cannot be authenticated but his narrative portrait might well be titled "Salus Populi Romani," for in it he presents to us Jesus, the Savior of the world. Mary is portrayed by Luke as the first and totally faithful disciple of Jesus, and it is from her that we learn what our own discipleship must be.

These motifs of *Journey*, *Universal Salvation* and *Discipleship* re-echo throughout the entire Gospel. But their first quiet heralding comes in the Infancy Narrative (Chapters 1 and 2) which has never failed to capture and delight Christian hearts. Shining through these themes, like the undertone of a painting, is the pervasive presence of the Holy Spirit. All of this unfolds within the context of reflection and prayer of ordinary people going about the ordinary tasks of daily life.

Journey

> Happy are those who find refuge in you, whose hearts
> are set on pilgrim roads. (Ps 84:6)

Mary set out from Galilee to Judea to stay with her kinswoman, Elizabeth, and made the return trip three months later (Lk 1:39-56). When her pregnancy was close to term, she and Joseph traveled south again to register in Jerusalem for the world census (Lk 2:1-7). These had to have been arduous journeys for Mary whose condition was made more uncomfortable by Palestine's rugged land surfaces. Israel today remains a land of rocky hills and slopes traversed by dusty footpaths and roads strewn with rough stones.

Already this Gospel speaks to our hearts, telling us that our journey, like that of the Holy Infant in Mary's womb, begins even before our own feet can feel the earth beneath us. We are God-sent on this difficult road. Our walking staff is not clarity about the mission nor how it will be accomplished but, rather, faith in the One who sends us and for Whom "nothing will be impossible" (Lk 1:37). We are spared foreknowledge of trials and sorrows along the way, though experience tells us they must come. But with trust that says, "Let it be done to me according to your word" (Lk 1:38), each today can strengthen us for the remaining tomorrows.

The journey continues with Mary and Joseph returning to Galilee to devote themselves to their life together and to the Child as he grew from infancy and childhood to adolescence and manhood (Lk 2:40, 52). Our journey, too, is made in stages as we advance in human and spiritual experience. It is important to remember that "Abram journeyed on by stages" (Gn 12:9; 13:3) and that "the whole Israelite community journeyed by stages" to the Promised Land (Ex 17:1), for the spiritual geography of the Gospels is rooted in the First Testament where our story begins. Chapter 33 of the Book of Numbers opens with: "The following are the stages by which the Israelites journeyed...." It goes on to record not only the routes and campsites, but the types of terrain the ancestors trod on their way to the Promised Land: through the sea (v. 8); to a place of springs and palm trees (v. 9); into the desert (vv. 11, 14, 15); up the mountains (vv. 23, 32, 37); on the plains (v. 48). Wherever their paths led them, the Lord was with the people, by day and by night, "in all the stages of their journey" (Ex 40:38).

According to Jewish custom, the Holy Family went to Jerusalem every year to remember in celebration and ritual how God "passed over" the blood-marked doorposts of their ancestors, starting them on their journey (Lk 2:41-50; cf. Ex 11-12:1-36). During a particular one of these Passover pilgrimages, a blood-stained cross would mark the end of Jesus' earthly journey, and from that time on would be the sign of every Christian's destiny.

We walk with Jesus on a road that follows the changing terrain, all the while making (our) way toward Jerusalem (cf. Lk 13:22). But strength and joy — Amen! and Alleluia! — accompany us with this reminder from the empty tomb: "Remember — he spoke to you when he was still in Galilee and said that the Son of Man would have to be handed over into the hands of sinners, and be crucified, and rise on the third day" (Lk 24:6, 7). The Apostle Paul remembered — and bequeathed us this guideline:

> I strain toward the goal to win the prize — of God's heavenward call in Christ Jesus.... Let us conduct ourselves in the light of what we've already attained. (Ph 3:14, 16)

It is likely that the two disciples on their way to Emmaus were having second thoughts about continuing along the course they had been on. They were already well into their seven mile trek out of Jerusalem when Jesus, in unfamiliar appearance, approached and began to walk along with them. To his question, "What have you been discussing on *your* way?" (instead of *his* way), they refer sadly to Jesus of Nazareth, "a prophet mighty in word and deed." As the conversation continues, it is the power of Jesus' word that prompts them to press him to remain with them. And when the three are seated together at table, it is in the power of Jesus' deed that they recognize him. Immediately they return to their Jerusalem community and recount "what had happened on the road and how they had recognized him in the breaking of the bread" (Lk 24:13-35).

The Word spoken, the Bread broken: Scripture and Eucharist are our food for the journey. In Holy Word, in Holy Bread, Jesus stays with us, touching our hearts which burn within to make us aware of his presence on the road.

Salvation for All

> People will come from the east and the west, from the north and the south, and will recline at table in the Kingdom of God. (Lk 13:29)

The first sounding of the universal salvation theme in Luke occurs at the angel's announcement to Mary that she would bear a son who is to be called Jesus (Lk 1:31) — a name which means, "God saves." John the Baptist begins his mission by proclaiming that the long-awaited One would fulfill Isaiah's prophecy: "All flesh shall see the salvation of God" (Lk 3:6). Finally, while Matthew had emphasized for his Jewish audience the Jewish roots of Jesus, now Luke — for his Gentile audience — traces the genealogy back to Adam to identify Jesus with the whole human race (Lk 3:23-38). God had chosen the Jews from among all the nations on earth to be "my special possession, dearer to me than all other people, though all the earth is mine" (Ex 19:5). Now, even more wondrously, the God who loved Israel into a people set apart (Dt 7:6-8), had become one of them to save all peoples from their sins.

People are the most important element in the human experience of life. Luke's Jesus singles out individual men and women of all types and categories to teach that his salvation is all-inclusive. How did Jesus approach people and interact with them? What was their response to him? It is through these encounters that Luke refines his Jesus-portrait. With hearts attentive to these stories, we can learn more about ourselves as well, and about how we relate to those we meet on the road.

The Twelve

At the outset of his ministry, Jesus invited twelve men (mostly fishermen, all but one from Galilee) to be the first to join him in community. So strong was his appeal that they asked no questions but followed him without hesitation.

Jesus inspired an awareness in these men of the deeper meaning of their ordinary lives. They remained with him because of what was happening as a result of their relationship with him: he brought out the best in them and they were growing in self-knowledge; they saw that together with him, they could do much more than they could accomplish on their own; they rarely really understood all that he said, so they discovered the value of friendship and discussion among themselves; he treated them with honesty, fairness, understanding and love, and opened their eyes to human needs all around them; he trusted them with responsibility and they sensed that they were an important part of his ministry.

Above all, he taught them the need for prayer, both as a practice and as an attitude that relates life to God. They responded to him with dedication and eventually (with the exception of the despairing Judas), they carried his message to places where Jesus himself had never walked.

The Women

We meet more women in Luke-Acts than in any other Gospel. Women felt liberated by Jesus because he respected them as persons in their own right; he understood their needs and valued the things they did; he helped them to appreciate themselves and their special gifts and to discover their even greater potential. Jesus had close women friends and encouraged female disciples to join him on the road.

All of this was counter to the Jewish tradition and attitude of his day which had little regard for the social and legal status of women. For their part, women responded to Jesus by becoming his followers, by ministering to his needs, by total loyalty when others fled. They were the first to receive and to believe the message from the empty tomb — and the first to be sent to proclaim the Good News to others.

The Strangers and Unfortunate Ones

In Chapter 6 of Luke's Gospel we stop at a stretch of level land along the road and hear Jesus give a summary discourse which parallels Matthew's Sermon on the Mount. Here, in addition to blessings for those who are poor, hungry, grieving and persecuted for their faith, Jesus has stern warnings for those whose self-interest causes such misery. Woe to you who are rich, indulgent, laughing and held in great esteem now — if you fail to treat others as you like to be treated yourselves!

Jesus seeks out and welcomes the neglected and defenseless ones, giving them a new self-image and hope for improving their situations. Because Jesus lives what he preaches, he reveals in his own character the qualities by which Christians must bear witness to God's saving love: gentleness, compassion, forgiveness, generosity, humility, joy, prayerfulness.

If the Word of God has come into the world for the salvation of all people, then the saving message of God's Word must be proclaimed for all. As the road unfolds before us, it puts us in touch with people whose lives are very different from our own: persons of other races, nationalities and religions, as well as those of no religious belief at all. Prejudging others because of ethnic origin and customs, creed, gender and similar circumstances of birth and learning is contrary to the world's great religions and is certainly foreign to the teaching and example of Jesus of Galilee. But where is the Christian, or any human being, who has no need to unlearn the personal prejudices he or she has acquired along the way? It took a vision to convince Peter that God's Spirit was as much at work in the

Gentiles not bound by Jewish circumcision and dietary laws as
in the lives of the Chosen People who did observe these pre-
scriptions. Peter's strange vision was linked with another vision
granted to the centurion, Cornelius. Their coupled experiences
prepared Peter to shed his own religious bias and paved the way
for Gentiles to be admitted to the Christian community. The
details of Peter's enlightenment are recorded by Luke in Chapter 10 of Acts. With his own vision widened, Peter formulates
the only acceptable Christian and human attitude toward those
whose ways are foreign to our own: "Now I truly see that God
does not play favorites. Instead, those of every nation who fear
Him and do what is right are acceptable to Him" (Acts 10:34,
35).

Along the way we encounter the poor and the sick, sinners and criminals, the displaced and forgotten ones of this
world. If we can acknowledge and remember that in some way
we, too, are among these wretched of the earth, we are blessed
indeed. For then we experience the compassion of Jesus as spoken to us in our own need: "Your sins are forgiven" (Lk 7:48);
"The least of all of you is the greatest" (Lk 9:48); "Woman,
you have been set free of your illness" (Lk 13:12); "Stand up
and go; your faith has saved you" (Lk 17:19); "Amen, I say to
you: this day you will be with me in Paradise" (Lk 23:43).

Discipleship

I will show you what someone is like who comes to
me, listens to my words, and acts on them. (Lk 6:47)

Mary said to the angel: "Behold, the handmaid of the Lord. Let it be done to me according to your word" (Lk 1:38). With this acceptance of God's Word into her heart, Mary becomes the first disciple of Jesus and the model of discipleship for us. With her "yes" she begins to act upon the Word she has received. Mary hastens to share the Word of God with Elizabeth who receives it with great joy and responds in confirming gratitude: "Blessed is she who believed that there would be a fulfillment of what was spoken to her by the Lord" (Lk 1:45).

It is in Luke's Gospel more than any other that the person of Mary shines through. His scriptural image of her is a masterpiece in which, with lines ever so delicate, he depicts a woman of great inner strength. Two qualities in Mary teach us how to travel the road as faithful followers of Jesus. The first is to receive and treasure God's Word in our hearts. Mary had questions: "How can this be?" (Lk 1:34). She had fears: "This child... is a sign that will be opposed — and a sword will pierce your own soul" (Lk 2:34, 35). She did not grasp the meaning of her life's experiences: "Son, why did you do this to us? You see that your father and I have been searching for you, worried to death" (Lk 2:48). Like us, Mary did not understand how, through the unexpected and painful circumstances of her life, God's will was being accomplished. We may well imagine that Mary sometimes prayed as we so often do: "Dear God, what is it that you want me to do? Please show me the way." But the memories Mary treasured and reflected on in her heart (Lk 2:51) would sustain her faith and mature her intercessions before God. More likely, her prayer would have been: "Keep me on your path, O God, wherever it may lead." For Mary believed in God's

love for her (Lk 1:28), in God's promises to her (Lk 1:45) —
and that was enough. She did not have to understand now. She
did not have to be shown the way. Quietly but steadfastly, Mary
followed her Son through his ministry and death, and after his
ascension she was an important and revered presence in the
gatherings of the young Church (Acts 1:14).

The second quality of discipleship we learn from Mary is
to act upon the Word, to fulfill God's will as it is revealed to us
through the people, places and events we encounter along the
way. This is what Jesus accomplished by his life, death and resurrection. Those who follow in his Way can do no less, for God's
message to us is clear:

> So shall my word be
> that goes forth from my mouth;
> it shall not return to me void,
> but shall do my will,
> achieving the end for which I sent it.
> (Isaiah 55:11)

Luke records two separate occasions when Jesus holds his
mother up as one who hears the Word of God and acts upon
it. Once when the crowds were so great that Mary and some
other family members were unable to get through to him, he
was informed that they were outside. "You, too, are my family," he said in effect to the crowd, "if you, like they, hear the
word of God and put it into practice in your lives" (See Lk 8:19-
21).

Another time when he was speaking to a large group, a
woman who was impressed with what he had to say shouted out,

"Blessed is the womb that bore you and the breasts at which you nursed." He responded with even higher praise for his mother. More than for her maternal protection and nourishment in childhood, Jesus loved Mary for what she taught him by her life: to receive God's Word into one's heart and to live the truth of that Word throughout life's journey (Lk 11:27, 28).

Luke-Acts is an exciting and adventuresome account of the Spirit at work in the early Church. At the same time, it leaves no doubt about the road's changing terrain nor about the cost of the Christian journey. It seems appropriate that the Acts narrative should come to an abrupt and unfinished ending — for this is *our* story being told and we are still pilgrims on the road.

For Your Meditation...

ON A TREE FALLEN ACROSS THE ROAD

The tree the tempest with a crash of wood
Throws down in front of us is not to bar
Our passage to our journey's end for good,
But just to ask us who we think we are

Insisting always on our own way so.
She likes to halt us in our runner tracks
And make us get down in a foot of snow
Debating what to do without an ax.

And yet she knows obstruction is in vain:
We will not be put off the final goal
We have it hidden in us to attain,
Not though we have to seize earth by the pole.

And, tired of aimless circling in one place,
Steer straight off after something into space.

Robert Frost (1874-1963)

**Make known to me your ways, LORD;
teach me your paths.
(Psalm 25:4)**

7

Alone in the Desert

I will lead her into the desert and speak to her heart.
(Hosea 2:16)

Contrary to popular belief, sand is not the predominant feature of the deserts of planet earth. More correctly, these terrains differ widely due to natural processes over long periods of time. Gravity, weathering, rainfall and wind activity have created such varied desert forms as mountains and plateaus, sand sheets and volcanic peaks, plains and craters, dry lakes and river beds. The common elements by which these different terrains are classified as desert or wilderness are: environmental extremes of heat and cold, scarcity or lack of water and sparse to non-existent vegetation. These conditions make any kind of populous habitation impossible except by artificial means.

Three diverse arid regions make up more than half of Israel's total land surface: the Judean Desert — a barren mountain wilderness comprising the eastern slopes of Judea; the Arava Valley — a savannah region between the Dead Sea and Eilat containing scattered trees and drought-resistant undergrowth;

and the Negev — the loess flatlands of buff to gray fine-grained silt or clay and limestone mountains of southern Israel where only desert scrub brush grows.

But had not God promised the chosen people "a land flowing with milk and honey"? It was to Moses that God first described the Promised Land in terms of its indigenous prosperity (Ex 3:8). The description was passed on to succeeding generations and preserved throughout the Hebrew Scriptures (e.g., Nb 14:8; Dt 26:9; Jr 11:5; Si 46:8). When Israel was in exile centuries later, God would further enhance that original imagery through the prophet Ezekiel who referred to the land of milk and honey as "a jewel among all lands" (Ezk 20:15).

Even so, centuries of pilgrims who have since sojourned through the Holy Land's desert places — whether by actual travel or through reflective Scripture reading — have paused to query: "Does this land really measure up to God's pledge?" (When over fifty per cent of an already small piece of land is of itself desolate, some question about its unsurpassed value does not seem unreasonable.) The very question can awaken us to the reality that nowhere is the Bible more our story than in the desert experiences of life.

Harmony of the Testaments

As we travel the spiritual geography of the Gospels, we become increasingly aware of the unity of the two Testaments. While the life, death and resurrection of Jesus is the focus of the New Testament, Christian memory reaches back to its Old Testament roots and especially to the desert origins of the chosen people. It was in the desert that they were called to be God's covenant community and it was through the desert that God led them from slavery to freedom in the land of promise.

For Christians, too, the desert is our meeting place with God, particularly in times of crisis. It is there — in pain and in struggle — that we discern our own identity as individuals and as Church. It is not surprising then that our sense of shared history is set in sharpest relief in the desert. For Christians, as well as for their Hebrew ancestors, all the way to the Promised Land is through the desert.

Indeed, it is in the wilderness that we most readily recognize as our own the motif that recurs throughout the entire Old Testament: *Sin—Forgiveness—Repentance—Reconciliation.* The inspired Hebrew authors remembered with remarkable candor the repeated infidelities of God's chosen people in the desert. Discontent, grumbling, internal strife, disobedience, rebellion, idol worship: all this and more is openly acknowledged and preserved. Perhaps we have read these accounts wondering what it would have taken for this "stiff-necked people" to trust in a God whose presence and providence were never wanting. But as we travel the dry and barren deserts of life — allowing the land to speak to our hearts — perhaps we can begin to hear in their grumbling complaints and insolent questions our own forgetfulness, our own ingratitude, our own lack of trust:

> Why did you bring us out here to die in the desert?
> (Ex 14:11)
> What are we to drink? (Ex 15:24)
> Is the LORD in our midst or not? (Ex 17:7)

Come, make us a god who will be our leader. (Ex
32:1)
We are famished; we see nothing before us but this
manna. (Nb 11:6)

These grumblings translate easily into our own "why me?"
and "how come?" and "Is this all there is to life?" In the midst
of our pain and struggle, we can fail to perceive the desert as a
place of holy encounter with God. We survey the landscape
formed by fear, sorrow, illness, doubt, betrayal, rejection and
find ourselves asking: Does this land really measure up to God's
promises? Where is God in this forsaken land?

The desert is a harsh place and a place of hard questions.
As we grow in recognition of the Bible as our own story, we
begin to understand that these difficult questions (which we
often mutter as complaints and pleas to God) are the seeds of
desert insights. Over and again in the Scriptures God speaks to
our worries, fears, frustrations and uncertainties: You are not
alone. I am with you. I will lead you where you are to go and I
will show you what you are to do. You are mine and I love you.
Do not be afraid. These are the sure answers of faith that sustain and support us in the midst of the desert. The real question is: Do we believe them? If we can learn to embrace God's
Word in response to the honest questions that bewilder us, then
we can walk with unshakable confidence, even when the road
stretches through unfamiliar or hostile territory.

Moses in the Desert

Among the Old Testament personages who awaken us to this truth is Israel's greatest prophet and teacher, Moses, whose whole life was a desert experience. Hear the dialogue that takes place as Moses stands on holy ground and attempts to dissuade God from placing upon him the burdens of a mission he would prefer not to have:

MOSES: Who am I that I should lead the Israelites out of Egypt? (Ex 3:11)

GOD: I will be with you. (Ex 3:12)

MOSES: What am I to tell them when they ask me God's name? (Ex 3:13)

GOD: Tell them "I AM" sent me to you. (Ex 3:14)

MOSES: Suppose they will not believe me, nor listen to my plea? (Ex 4:1)

GOD: Certain signs will take place so that they may believe. (Ex 4: 2-9)

MOSES: I have never been eloquent... I am slow of speech and tongue. (Ex 4:10)

GOD: I will assist you in speaking and teach you what to say. (Ex 4:12)

MOSES: If you please, Lord, send someone else! (Ex 4:13)

GOD: Go! Aaron will help you and I will assist you both. (Ex 4:14-16)

In each instance, Moses hears his questions and objections return to him as insights of faith. God had initiated this conversation with Moses from within a bush in the desert which, though totally ablaze with fire, remained unscorched. This

magnificent image symbolizes for Moses and for us the role of
faith in our earthly life and mission. Though trials and hard-
ships accompany our efforts, these shall not consume us (Ex
3:1-3). Though we are encompassed by doubts and feelings of
inadequacy, we must know that it is God's work we are about
and God who will accomplish it through us. God's final word
to Moses in this encounter is also meant for our ears and hearts:
"Take this staff [of faith] in your hand; with it you are to perform the signs" (Ex 4:17).

The Hebrew Scriptures remind the people of both Testaments of our common infidelities to the One God who, nevertheless, remains faithful and forgiving. For the Christian, not
only does this theme come to redemptive fruition in the Paschal Mystery of Jesus, but it is precisely in light of his passion,
death and resurrection that the Old Testament takes on its full-
est meaning.

In the New Testament Gospels, the proclamation of God's
Kingdom on earth comes forth from the wilderness — first in
the voice of the last and greatest of Old Testament prophets,
John the Baptist, and finally in the advent and mission of Jesus,
the Christ. God's plan that these two lives be so closely paral-
leled warrants our special attention, for together they hold the
key to the significance of the desert in Christian understanding
and growth.

John the Baptist's Desert Vocation

All four Gospel accounts present John as the fulfillment
of the prophecy of Isaiah:

"A voice of one crying out in the desert:
    'Prepare the way of the LORD,
    make straight his paths'"
(Mk 1:3; Mt 3:3; Lk 3:4; Jn 1:23; cf. Is 40:3). In a sense, John is a kind of advance man for the Lord — like one who precedes and indicates the imminent approach of an important personage. But there is a deeper reality to John's role in the desert that we must not fail to grasp — first, because it gives meaning to the deserts of our own lives; and, secondly, because his is the mission of every Christian.

Before John's conception, the Angel Gabriel announced God's assignment for him with succinct clarity: "to prepare a people made perfect for the Lord" (Lk 1:17). God had already prepared the way —through the Law, through the Prophets, through the Land — for salvation to be made known on earth. Then, at the divinely appointed time, "the word of God came to John the son of Zechariah in the desert. He came to the whole region around the Jordan, proclaiming a baptism of repentance for the forgiveness of sins..." (Lk 3:2, 3). John was called forth from the desert to dispose a people to receive their Savior, to turn their hearts away from sin and towards the Awaited One, Jesus of Galilee. He preached this good news to the people, exhorting them with concrete examples of how they would need to change their lives and especially their manner of relating to others (cf. Lk 3:10-18).

The written accounts are generous with details about the Baptist. Among other things, we know how he dressed and what he ate (Mk 1:6; Mt 3:4). We see John as one who could proclaim the truth reproachfully (Mt 3:7-12) or with sincere humility (Jn 1:19-34) as the situation warranted. We are touched by the affection and esteem with which Jesus speaks of John (Mk 11:27-33; Mt 11:7-15; Jn 5:33-35). And we have a graphic description of the dramatic climax of Herod's birthday party — nothing less than the presentation to a young dancing girl of John's severed head on a platter (Mk 6:17-29)! All of this makes John a particularly interesting and colorful figure. But more importantly, as the Gospels disclose the person and mission of John in the desert, we imbibe something of the nature and significance of the desert in our own lives.

The desert requires us to travel lightly, leaving behind not only our customary indulgences but often those things we consider essential as well. Faced with lack of resources, we recognize the need to depend on God for sustenance, for protection, for a sense of direction and purpose. Whether the sojourn be prolonged or brief, it is a time of seemingly endless waiting that exercises one's patience to a purifying degree. But faith produces perseverance (Jm 1:3), and trials strengthen our hope (Rm 5:1-5). The inner wisdom of God's Spirit touches our hearts by way of mysterious contradictions: we experience weakness that strengthens, darkness that illumines, silence that speaks, death that gives birth to new life. Called forth from the desert, we find the courage to embrace — whether clearly or only vaguely defined — the next stage for which we are being readied. *WE are the people being made perfect for the Lord!* And even while our own preparation continues, we are already commissioned to prepare others to open their hearts to Jesus of Galilee (Jn 1:29-51).

Jesus and the Desert

Christian spirituality, we have noted, is anchored in the oneness of the Paschal Mystery of Jesus. To live the Christian life is to enter into the experience of both death and resurrection. It is to embrace both *Amen* ("So be it!") and *Alleluia* ("Praise God!"). Twenty centuries of Christian faith rest on this fundamental truth, relayed from the empty tomb and sublimely expressed in a hymn used in very early Church liturgies. Paul incorporates this Christological hymn into his captivity letter to the church at Philippi:

> Have the same outlook among you that Christ Jesus had,
> Who, though he was in the form of God,
> > did not consider equality with God
> > something to hold on to.
> Instead, he emptied himself and took on
> > the form of a slave,
> > born in human likeness;
> > and to all appearances a man.
> He humbled himself and became obedient,
> > even unto death, death on a cross.
> For this reason God exalted him
> > and gave him a name above every
> > other name,
> So that at the name of Jesus every knee shall bend,
> > in the heavens, on earth, and below the earth,
> And every tongue will proclaim to the glory
> > of God the Father,
> > that Jesus Christ is Lord... (Ph 2:5-11).

This hymn has been called the Christian formula for greatness. It extols and celebrates the crucified and risen Jesus precisely as he exemplifies the desert as essential to our story. "Go to Galilee" is the message we have received. Accepting that directive to embrace our lives as Jesus did his means following him wherever the road takes us. Inevitably, it will lead us through the desert any number of times and by routes that defy human understanding. These will never be comfortable experiences and may even seem to us to be unfortunate, off-course wanderings that impede our journey's progress.

But life demands patience, a virtue that can be developed only by being put to the test. This requires us to pass through the vast wilderness of waiting — for God's call to be heard, for God's hour to come, for God's will to be made manifest and accomplished. Gradually, we come to understand the need for self-discipline and, ultimately, for obedience unto death. Our desert experiences, then, become occasions for God's favor for it is the emptying of self that enables us to be filled with God's merciful love.

We are told that as Jesus' reputation spread and the crowds he ministered to grew larger, he often retired to desert places to pray (Lk 5:15,16). On one such occasion as Jesus was returning from prayer, one of his disciples pressed him to teach them how to pray. What was there in his eyes and demeanor that revealed to them the lingering effects of his communion in prayer with the Father? Whatever it was they observed spoke to them of a spirit they would like to share. Jesus responded by teaching them not only how to pray, but also of the need to pray perseveringly and of the effects they could expect from their prayer. If they would but ask, not only would they share his prayerful spirit, but they would be given the abiding presence of God's Holy Spirit (Lk 11:1-13). The very loneliness of the desert makes it a place of intimate prayer. In blessed solitude we discover that we have not been, nor are we now, alone. Rather, we find ourselves alone with the Living God who speaks to our hearts and consoles us in our need.

Paradoxically, the desert is also a place of promise and of hope. The barrenness of Israel's Judean wilderness may easily evoke feelings of sadness, even depression, in the pilgrim traveler. However, it is precisely the hard, arid surface of this wasteland that holds the secret hope of spring! The winter rainfall in this desert, which is minimal at best, cannot be absorbed by the sun-parched land. The result is phenomenal flooding which causes the desert to bloom in springtime with exquisite wild flowers, grasses and bushes of tamarisk. Isaiah's poetic description of the return of God's People from exile most surely was inspired by the sensual delight of the Judean Desert in bloom. Read this beautiful interpretive scene in Chapter 35 of Isaiah and you will find yourself returning to it frequently. Through the imagery of the land, it describes the fulfillment of God's promises to those who embrace life in all of its terrains. Most especially is it a passage to ponder in the desert: God's Word for our own times of exile in the wilderness.

For Your Meditation...

THE DESERT WILL BLOOM
[From Isaiah 35]

The desert and the parched land will exult;
the steppe will rejoice and bloom.
They will bloom with abundant flowers:
and rejoice with joyful song....
Streams will burst forth in the desert,
and rivers in the steppe
The burning sands will become pools,
and the thirsty ground, springs of water:
A highway will be there,
called the holy way;...
It is for those with a journey to make,
and on it the redeemed will walk....
They will meet with joy and gladness,
sorrow and mourning will flee.

**The LORD your God has blessed you in all your undertakings;
He has been concerned about your journey
through this vast desert.
(Dt 2:7)**

8

Together in Jerusalem

I rejoiced when they said to me,
"Let us go to the house of the LORD."
And now our feet are standing
within your gates, Jerusalem. (Ps 122:1, 2)

Most pilgrims to Israel arrive at Ben-Gurion Airport located near Lod, seven miles from Tel Aviv on the highway to Jerusalem. The motor trip to the capital by bus, car or sherut (shared taxi) is another thirty some miles which become a steep climb before the city comes into view. Along the way, road signs in Hebrew, Arabic and English announce that the Golden City is now only a short distance away. But it is the pull of the vehicle changing gear to accommodate the sharply rising road that quickens one's anticipation. This upward thrust of forward motion is for many their initial spiritual experience of the land — a breath-catching realization of the same ascent made by ancient Israelites and by Jesus of Galilee and the people of his time.

One always goes "up" to Jerusalem which is situated in the central mountain range of the country. It is built upon and surrounded by hills and valleys with names that are familiar to even less than avid Bible readers: e.g., Mount Sion, Mount Moriah, Mount of Olives, Kidron Valley. The original city conquered by King David circa 1,000 BCE (Before the Christian Era) lies outside the southeastern corner of the Temple Mount. The site, excavated and restored in part from the multi-layered ruins of successive conquests, is now an archaeological park open to the public.

Today's Old City of Jerusalem is the outgrowth of the original site, extended and changed many times throughout the history that is buried beneath it. Its streets — narrow, winding and unevenly paved — support dwellings, markets, shops and religious sanctuaries. The traffic is dense with people of cosmopolitan features, languages, dress and customs together with animals (goats and donkeys, for example), wagons and vending carts. Emanating from this conglomeration are the smells: some unpleasant odors, to be sure, but also the aromas of unusual and delicious foods (still in the cooking process or enticingly displayed within close reach), and the fragrance of exotic spices and incense. Rising from all of this are the sounds. Given the components of the mixture just described, one should expect the sounds to be as varied and as noisy as, in fact, they are.

This Old City is compacted into an area of about one-third of a square mile, or one square kilometer. It is surrounded by stone walls dating from the sixteenth century which roughly follow the course of those the Romans built around Jerusalem in the second century. These walls have seven gates of entry besides the now sealed Golden Gate through which, according to Jewish tradition, the Messiah will enter in triumph.

But the walls cannot contain modern Jerusalem which stretches like the microscopic amoeba beyond the Old City to its environs. Here twentieth century art, architecture and technology have transformed the ravaged and neglected wasteland of previous centuries into a beautiful New City. Such diverse structures as the Knesset, the Shrine of the Book, the Hadassah-Hebrew University Hospital and Synagogue and the poignant Yad Vashem Holocaust Memorial all blend aesthetic principles with those of utility and function. The fourth and most unifying element of such contemporary buildings is the unique religious history of the Jewish people. Throughout their Scriptures, they are instructed and warned by the prophets to keep in memory the events that forged them into a people set apart: "...take care and be earnestly on your guard not to forget the things which your own eyes have seen, nor let them slip from your memory as long as you live, but teach them to your children and to your children's children" (Dt 4:9). Indeed, these memories perdure and find expression today in all facets of life in the modern city of Jerusalem.

Israel's most sacred rememberings, however, are enshrined within the Old City, where the Western (retaining) Wall is all that remains of the Temple destroyed by Titus in 70 CE (Christian Era). To this holiest place of prayer, Jews the world over come to remember and to grieve over the loss of their Temple, but also to celebrate and mourn the events of their own lives. Similar sentiments mark our entry into Jerusalem, for the symbolism of this city and its Temple are at the very heart of the Christian story.

From biblical and related sources, it is possible to com-

pile a long list of descriptive names for Jerusalem — perhaps as
many as the perfect Hebrew number of seventy! Two seem most
significant for Christian faith and spirituality and of these, one
has been stressed at several places in our travel thus far:

Jerusalem,
The City of Destiny

Our pilgrimage through the spiritual geography of the land
began by remembering the day of Jesus' death and the resplen-
dent morning of his resurrection. Both the hill of Calvary where
Jesus was crucified and the burial tomb from which he arose
are enclosed within the Church of the Holy Sepulchre in Old
Jerusalem. Historical and archaeological evidence leave little
doubt about the authenticity of this holiest and most vener-
ated shrine of Christendom. Ironically, the perpetuation of these
sites is attributable not only to those who revered the holy
places, but also to those who wanted to obliterate all memories connected with them. Both have served to mark and pro-
tect the exact locations! In the process, however, any resem-
blance to the hill and tomb of the Gospels, or as depicted in
art through the ages, is now well hidden from view. Still, the
truth remains: the final journey of Jesus makes it possible for
us to "go to Galilee" — to embrace our lives as we continue
toward the city of his destiny and ours.

It is to us that Jesus announces, "We are going up to
Jerusalem" (Mk 10:33). It is together that we journey to our
destiny — that is, in the presence of our God and in company
with one another. Both concepts are central to the image of

the Temple which bestows upon the city a second name for our consideration:

Jerusalem,
The Mountain of the Lord's House

When Solomon had completed the magnificent edifice that took seven years to build, he and the entire community of Israel assembled for the dedication. After the ark of the covenant was placed by the priests within the holy of holies, "the LORD's glory [presence] filled the Temple" (1 K 8:10, 11). The God who had been content to dwell in a cloth tent pitched in the desert, now graciously accepted this more elaborate abode:

> I have consecrated this temple which you have built;
> I confer my name upon it forever, and my eyes and
> my heart shall be there always. (1 K 9:3)

These are strange promises when one considers the adverse history of the Temple. The periods of building and rebuilding, renovation and expansion all ended in destruction, abandonment, desecration and total ruin. There has been no Temple in Jerusalem since the first century. How, then, could God promise to remain within the Temple — personally ("my name"), watchfully ("my eyes"), lovingly ("my heart") — and forever?

Patiently God teaches us through the Scriptures that "so high are my ways above your ways, and my thoughts above your thoughts" (Is 55:9). We do not easily understand that so often we "are thinking not as God does, but as human beings do"

(Mk 8:33). Divine inspiration had prompted David's desire to
build a fitting dwelling place for the Lord. But when David
expressed his wish, God responded with:

> I have not dwelt in a house from the day on which I
> led the Israelites out of Egypt to the present, but I
> have been going about in a tent under cloth. In all
> my wanderings... did I ever utter a word... to ask:
> Why have you not built me a house of cedar? (2 S
> 7:6, 7)

Nevertheless, God allowed this human dream to be pursued and
realized — not by David but by Solomon, his son. The deeper
promise, however, was made to David to whom was revealed
God's own building plans: It is I, rather, who will establish a
house for you! I will fix a place for my people Israel! (See 2 S
7:10-13).

There is an important lesson here. Our human dreams and
plans, be they ordinary or grandiose, are temporal, "for our city
here is not a lasting one; we seek the city that is to come" (Heb
13:14). At the same time, God inspires and respects our dreams
and plans, for through them the unfolding of the divine intention for us is communicated. God's will can come to light in
realized or forsaken dreams — and through plans fulfilled, frus-
trated, postponed or wrecked. When we learn to recognize the
diversity of God's ways, then we are in touch with a God "who
is able to do so much more than all we can ask for or imagine,
by the power at work within us" (Eph 3:20).

The destruction of Jerusalem and of Solomon's Temple
was foretold by the Old Testament prophets (e.g., Jr 7:1-15;

Mi 3:12). A second Temple to replace the destroyed original was begun in 537 and dedicated in 515 BCE by the remnant Jews returning from Babylonian Exile. Its structure had nothing of the grandeur of Solomon's edifice but it withstood the test of durability until 19 BCE when Herod the Great undertook to renovate and expand it as part of a massive building program. Ostensibly, the new Temple complex was a magnanimous gift to the Jews but more to the point, it served to further Herod's own political security.

It was this Second Temple that figured so prominently in the life and mission of Jesus. The buildings were finished and in use just a few years before the Savior's birth but their elaborate decorative features were not completed until AD 64. Just six years later, the Romans would sack Jerusalem and another magnificent Temple, built by human minds and hands, would be reduced to ashes and rubble.

A prophet for his own time and for all times, Jesus predicted this destruction of the Temple:

> As he was leaving the Temple one of his disciples said to him, "Teacher, look at how wonderful the stones and the buildings are!" Jesus said to him, "Do you see these great buildings? Not a stone will be left here upon a stone that will not be torn down" (Mk 13:1, 2; cf. Mt 24:1, 2; Lk 21:5, 6).

Seemingly, Jesus makes this prediction far more boldly in John's Gospel: "Destroy this Temple and in three days I will raise it up" (Jn 2:19)! "But," adds the evangelist in an explanatory comment characteristic of the fourth Gospel, "he was speaking about the Temple of his body" (Jn 2:21).

We begin to see that there are levels of meaning in Sacred Scripture. The human words which speak God's Word to us do so within the context of the entire Bible. For our ancestors in faith, the Jerusalem Temple was the symbol of God's presence among them. Jesus' reference to the Temple of his body which he would raise in three days, affirms God's presence in his resurrected body, the Church. Through baptism the Christian is incorporated into the community of Christ and becomes a living Temple:

> ...you are no longer strangers and aliens, but fellow citizens with the saints and members of God's household. You were built upon a foundation of apostles and prophets, and Christ Jesus himself was its cornerstone. In him the whole building is held together and grows into a holy Temple in the Lord; and in him you are being built together into God's dwelling place in the Spirit (Eph 2:19-22).

Now we can grasp how God's strange promise to David is wondrously fulfilled. *For WE are the house that God designs, builds and remains with forever — personally, watchfully and lovingly!*

Still, humans have always felt the need to honor their gods (and, through Israel, the One God) by erecting memorial markers and altars and by building temples, churches and shrines. God's presence is experienced in these places, not because of the structures themselves but because God chooses to dwell in the midst of the people gathered there in faith.

Although our places of pilgrimage and worship are temporal, they are of great importance. For while we reflect on Jerusalem as symbolizing the fulfillment of God's promises to us, the ongoing journey continues to require the attention and energy of heart and soul, mind and strength (Mk 12:28-34; Mt 22:34-40; Lk 10:25-28: cf. Dt 6:4-9). These energies are rekindled when Christians come together to offer praise and thanksgiving, sacrifice and petition to the God who journeys with us.

While each of us is called to holiness in uniquely individual fashion, our common vocation is to become a people, to establish community, to live as one family of God. It is through the richness of the Church's liturgical and sacramental life that this unity is effected and that we are most especially fitted for the task. Commemoration of the yearly cycle of seasons, feasts and ordinary time of Jesus' life strengthens our own faith and encourages the faith of those who walk with us in the footsteps of our crucified and risen Lord. Celebration of the Sacraments — all of which are social in nature — nourishes, heals and builds up the Body of Christ. Thus, we are mutually heartened and supported by an integrated spirituality grounded in the Word of God — and with the assurance that we travel together on the uphill road to Jerusalem, our destiny.

> Come let us climb the LORD's mountain...
> that we may be instructed in his ways
> and we may walk in God's paths....
> Come, let us walk in the light of the LORD!
>
> (Isaiah 2:3, 5)

For Your Meditation...

THE NEW JERUSALEM

Then I saw a new heaven and a new earth —
    the first heaven had passed away and the sea was no more.
And I saw the holy city, new Jerusalem,
      coming down out of heaven from God,
      prepared as a bride is adorned for her husband.

Then I heard a loud voice from the throne say,
      "Behold, God's dwelling is now with men.
He shall dwell with them and they shall be His people,
      and God Himself will be with them.
He'll wipe every tear from their eyes and death shall be no
more—
      no more grief or crying or pain,
      for what came before has passed away."

Then the One seated on the throne said,
      "Behold, I'll make all things new."

(Rv 21:2-5)

**O God, within your temple
we ponder your steadfast love.
(Ps 48:10)**

9

It is the Lord!

Now as day was breaking, Jesus stood there on the shore; but the disciples did not know that it was Jesus. (Jn 21:4)

Does it seem to you, as it does to me, that the journey has taken us far from the lovely scene at the Sea of Galilee where we began? We have been so engaged in climbing mountains and trying to follow the road wherever it leads. Our wanderings through the desert have been long and wearying. The ascent to Jerusalem continues daily and yearly, and attending to it with full heart and soul, mind and strength is not always easily accomplished.

It is time for us to go again to Galilee. You may recall an earlier suggestion of the need to return often to the sea and its shores, to a time when life was more simple and unencumbered by eventual responsibilities and burdens. That may seem a long while ago — as far back as childhood, perhaps, or to a time of major discovery, decision, commitment or change in your life.

We return to Galilee to remember the call of Jesus and our enthusiastic response to his invitation to walk through this life with him. It was his own enthusiasm that captured our hearts and drew us irresistibly to his ways, to his truth, to himself (Jn 14:6). We began to follow him before we knew the kind of courage it would take and to believe in him before realizing what the consequences would be. But it was also before we came to understand how much he really loves us.

There is no more compassionate expression of the love of Jesus for each of us than we find in the epilogue (Chapter 21) of John's Gospel. It is the story of the resurrection appearance at the Sea of Galilee (Tiberias) to seven of his disciples: Peter, Thomas, Nathaniel, James, John and "two others" not mentioned by name (vv. 1,2). It is the story, too, of our own reflective return to the Galilee of our life. If we watch and listen with our hearts to our story's retelling, we may get a glimpse of, and be surprised at, the spiritual growth that has taken place in us and in our companions on the journey. We may also sense a lack that needs to be filled for the maturing process to continue. Here we can recall how God has dealt with us in the past that we might better understand the present and find strength for our journey into the future. Most of all, we will experience the constancy and gentleness of God's love for us in every stage along the way.

(Please pause now and read John 21 from which the following reflections derive.)

Verse 1 — "Jesus revealed himself again to his disciples at the Sea of Galilee" (also called the Sea of Tiberias or Gennesareth). Jesus came to earth to enter wholeheartedly into our lives that we may have life in him. We have been on this road long enough to know the reality of his presence in all the experiences along the way. The memory of particular instances should be enough to enable us to set aside our present fears and worries and approach today with well-founded trust in his continued friendship: "I have called you friends, because everything I have heard from my Father I have made known to you" (Jn 15:15). But how often we forget to remember!

Verse 3 — "Simon Peter said to them, 'I am going fishing.' They said to him, 'We'll go with you, too.' So they went out and got into the boat...." It is evident from the Gospels that Jesus is most often to be found in the company of ordinary people — like these fishermen friends of his, and the one who is a tax collector, the women who journeyed with him, and many others — like ourselves. If we have ever wondered why these seem to be the ones he depends on most for spreading his message, perhaps it is because we are probably his best hope! The rich and the famous (with exceptions, to be sure) are too distracted by the "good life" to be witnesses to the Good News:

> How hard it is for those who are wealthy to enter the kingdom of God! It is easier for a camel to go through a needle's eye than for a rich person to enter the kingdom of God. (Lk 18:24, 25)

The poor and the downtrodden for whom Jesus has special compassion already have their mission in this life. "You always have the poor with you" (Mt 26:11), Jesus has said. Sadly, the poor may be the most effective witnesses to the love of Jesus in this world. To love means to will another's best good, to

enable another to become the fullness of the person God created. The very misery of these suffering ones calls forth, cries
out for, the best in the rest of humanity. It is they who offer us
the possibility of becoming our best selves — not, for the most
part, the other way around.

It is beyond human explanation why we ordinary folks are
privileged and commissioned to further God's kingdom on
earth. After all, we are prone to the same distractions and ob-
stacles of rich and poor alike! Nevertheless, Jesus chooses and
sends us forth to bear fruit through our love for one another
(Jn 15:16, 17).

Sometimes we need to experience the truth of Jesus' re-
mark, "...apart from me you can do nothing" (Jn 15:5). It is
easy enough to begin thinking of *my* work ("I am going
fishing") and *our* work ("We will go, too") when all the while
it is the *Lord's* work in which we share. Both "my" ministry and
"our" ministry are fruitless unless done in and through the Lord:
"...that night they caught nothing."

Verses 4-11 — "Now as dawn was breaking, Jesus stood
there on the shore; but the disciples did not know that it was
Jesus" (v. 4). We believe in the Lord's presence in this world
but we tend to overlook him in the most obvious person, place
or circumstance. While we seek elsewhere, Jesus is right there
on our own shore, where we are, with whom we are. Something unexpected and unexplainable may occur — an inspiration, a solution or a big catch of fish (vv. 5,6). On such occasions we are surprised anew with the sudden realization: "It is
the Lord!" (v. 7). Once again we are amazed, thrilled and

humbled that he makes us so necessary to himself, so vital to his work: "Bring some of the fish *you* just caught" (v. 10), he says. We comply (v. 11), knowing full well Whose power is really at work here. Jesus adds some of our fresh catch of fish to those already cooking on the glowing charcoal fire while nearby, a few loaves of bread are warming in its heat (v. 9). Can we imagine a more appealing scene than this cozy and intimate setting prepared for us at the lakeshore? It is the simplicity of Jesus' manner that is so attractive, his genuine delight in being with us again that enables us to be our most relaxed selves.

Verses 12, 13 — "'Come and eat breakfast.'... he came over and took the bread and gave it to them, and in like manner the fish." This is not our first invitation to a special meal with him and we cannot help but reminisce now about those other occasions. The setting of each situation has varied because of the location and time of day, the number of people present and his own intention at the time. Yet, in our memory there is a familiar oneness about them all. Each time since the first, we have thought of ourselves not as being invited to yet another feast, but rather as participating in the continuation of the same feast. It is the constant factor of His Presence that makes it so and that gives meaning to whatever time elapses between our gatherings.

There is an unmistakable connectedness, for example, between this seaside cookout at dawn and a meal we shared during Jesus' ministry with a much larger group of people at another spot beyond the water's edge. Again, Jesus was the gracious host and the menu consisted of fish and bread. Here, too, the food was miraculously increased to an overabundance (Mk 6:34-44; Mt 14:13-21; Lk 9:10-17; Jn 6:1-15). Not surprisingly, this repast takes our memories even further back to the daily provisions of quail and manna provided by God for our ancestors in the desert (Ex 16:4-15).

In like manner, we cannot miss the striking similarity between these meals and the Last Supper of Jesus. The former were by way of preparation for the latter at which Jesus himself becomes our food in the form of bread and wine. Jesus underscored the symbolism of the loaves and fishes by using the same introductory ritual for the multiplications as he used in the Upper Room for the institution of the Eucharist: he took bread, said the blessing, broke it, and gave it to us to eat. (Mk 6:41, 14:22; Mt 14:19, 26:26; Lk 9:16, 22:19; cf. 1 Cor 11:23, 24).

Verses 15-19 — With breakfast over, Jesus engages Peter in conversation in our presence, suggesting that the interaction is as much for our benefit as for Peter's. No mention is made of Peter's threefold denial (Mk 14:66-72; Mt 26:69-75; Lk 22:54-62; Jn 18:15-27), nor is there any expectation of an expression of remorse from him. Jesus who is well aware of what is in our hearts (Jn 2:24, 25; Acts 1:24, 15:8) knows that Peter had repented of his sin immediately after committing it. Indeed, the glow and warmth of the fire burning here on the shore had to be a painful reminder to him of that night when he stood warming himself by another charcoal fire as Jesus was being interrogated and beaten. Surely it is a chastened Peter who now lives the sentiments of the psalmist as his own: "For I know my offense; my sin is always before me" (Ps 51:5).

Jesus' intention here is to provide for us a model of the kind of loving forgiveness that must characterize our dealings with one another. Throughout the ministry, Jesus had taught by word and example what it means to be a truly forgiving person. There was the time, for example, that Peter questioned the Master about how often he was obliged to pardon one who had offended him. "As many as seven times?" Peter asked large-heartedly. "...not seven times but seventy-seven times," was the reply (Mt 18:21, 22). In other words, as many times as we are mistreated by another, that many times are we to extend forgiveness. Why? Because that is the measure of God's forgiveness towards us.

Here on the lakeshore, Jesus has just given Peter (and each of us who have in our own way abandoned him) a beautiful sign of his own forgiving heart by gathering us in friendship around a meal he himself prepared. Now he tells us that as his followers, we can do no less. Our forgiveness of one another must be as willing and as welcoming and find expression in loving service to one another: "Feed my lambs ... Tend my sheep ... Feed my sheep."

This whole incident reminds us once again of that final Passover meal with him. During that supper he had risen from the table, poured water into a basin and washed the feet of everyone there. Then he reclined at table once more and explained the meaning of his actions in these words:

> Do you understand what I have done for you? You call me 'teacher' and 'the Lord,' and rightly so, because I am. If I, therefore, the Lord and teacher, have washed your feet, you too, ought to wash one

another's feet. I have given you an example to follow, so that just as I have done for you, you should
also do. (Jn 13:12-15)

It was after this touching scene that Judas had gone out to
implement his betrayal plot. Jesus had been well aware of his
intention, just as he knew in advance that Peter was to deny
ever knowing him. But the imminent danger that Jesus sensed
did not prevent him from one more attempt to prepare us for
it. He spoke at length. But only after he had given his life and
risen from the tomb would we come to realize the depth of love
his words that night were meant to convey (Jn 14-16). He con-
cluded that memorable occasion in the upper room with the
tenderest of prayers, not only for us but also for those who
would come to know him through us (Jn 17).

Now back in Galilee, the risen Jesus continues to make
his presence known and to instruct us in his way of living this
life. For our part, we recognize within ourselves that we are
beginning to learn. At the Last Supper, Jesus had said to Peter,
"Where I am going, you cannot follow me now, but you will
follow later" (Jn 13:36). In vehement objection, Peter had de-
clared his readiness to lay down his life for the Master. Jesus
knew otherwise; but only when a rooster crowed in the darkness preceding the dawn of the next day, had Peter been con-
fronted with the weakness of his faith. Peter's faith has since
been strengthened by being put to the test and even by failing
the test. It is to this Peter of maturing faith — and to each of
us — that Jesus now repeats his original invitation: "Follow me."

From selections referred to in this epilogue chapter of John, we become aware that some of the most enlightening memories of the Person of Jesus are found in the Fourth Gospel. In fact, it is this element which most strikingly differentiates John's writings from the Synoptics whose greater emphasis is on the establishment of God's Kingdom on earth.

The Johannine Scriptures are a giant leap in first century understanding of the Person of Jesus. In one masterfully concise opening verse, John's Gospel presents the Jesus who has existed since before creation, who has a unique relationship with God, and who himself is God (1:1). In long narratives and discourses John further refines his description: Jesus *creates*, *redeems* and *renews* all that is. He *lights* the way, he *leads* the way, he *is* the *Way*. He is *Truth* that frees and *Life* eternal. He is life-giving *Bread* and quenching *Water*. He is the *Beginning* and *End* of all that is — and when his hour of glory is accomplished, his *Saving Spirit* enters the world to teach us everything and to remind us of all that he has said.

From John, then, a uniquely different portrait of Jesus emerges. From the beginning he is "I AM": he is God. But in choosing to walk the earth as one of us, he becomes The Word of God made flesh (Jn 1:14):

> ...what we have heard,
> what we have seen with our own eyes,
> what we have looked at
> and touched with our hands —
> we speak of the word of life.
>
> (1 Jn 1:1)

In John's Gospel the greatest commandment is exemplified in the testimony and example of Jesus' own life: "Love one another as I have loved you" (Jn 15:9-17). Discipleship in John is simply to believe in Jesus, that through our belief we may have life in his name.

For Your Meditation...

LIVING THE GOSPELS

So, then the Lord, after speaking to them, was raised up to Heaven and took his seat at the right hand of God. But they went out to proclaim the good news everywhere, the Lord working with them and confirming the word through the signs following upon it. (Mk 16:19-20).

Jesus came to them and spoke to them, saying: "All authority in Heaven and on earth has been given to me. Go, therefore, and make disciples of all nations, baptizing them in the name of the Father, and of the Son, and of the Holy Spirit, and teach them to observe all that I've commanded you and, behold, I'll be with you always, until the end of the age. (Mt 28:18-20).

Then he led them out to Bethany, and he lifted up his hands and blessed them. And it happened that as he was blessing them he parted from them and was carried up to Heaven. After they worshipped him they returned to Jerusalem with great joy, and they were constantly in the Temple, blessing God. (Lk 24:50-52).

Jesus also did many other signs in the presence of the disciples which are not written in this book, but these things have been written so that you may believe that Jesus is the Messiah, the Son of God, and so that by believing you may have life in his name. (Jn 20:30-31).

He took the five loaves and the two fish and, looking up to Heaven, he gave a blessing, and after breaking them he gave the loaves to his disciples and his disciples gave them to the crowds. (Mt 14:19)

10

To the Land We've Come

> Thus says the LORD:
> Stand beside the earliest roads,
> ask the pathways of old
> which is the way of good, and walk it;
> thus you will find rest for your souls.
>
> (Jr 6:16)

The geography of the land that is now modern day Israel has challenged individuals and nations physically, politically and spiritually since the most ancient of biblical times. It is the spiritual challenge that has been our focus here, for it is this land that produced the Holy Bible which in turn tells our divine-human story through the figurative language of the land.

We have seen that the varied terrains of this land communicate graphically to us a sense of its symbolism for our own life's journey. We can refine this awareness as we cultivate the habit of looking at our life as we travel through the land whenever we read the Sacred Scriptures. In our daily experiences and thoughts there are questions to ponder: Where am I now on my spiritual journey? What is this passage telling me about

myself, about my relationship to others and to God? To reflect
on the meaning (rather than on the why) of life's happenings
can open doors to new dimensions of one's continuing spiritual search and growth.

There is yet another source of awareness open to us as we
stand in the present and on the edge of the future. That, of
course, is remembering the past, of taking into account the
history that has brought us to this very moment in life. Someone once said, "The farther back you can look, the further ahead
you can see." There is wisdom in such an observation as well as
an implied suggestion that we might well take to heart. Without a doubt, we inhabit this earth at a fascinating period in
human history. The discoveries and advances made within our
lifetime have already radically changed life on our planet, both
for good and for evil. The future seems already here and hur-
tling forward at such a dizzying rate as to leave many of us with
a sense of scrambling to somehow catch up. As a result, while
we may be exhilarated by new possibilities already on our hori-
zon, we may at the same time experience anxiety over the unknown future of this fast-moving world. It is important to remind ourselves that this particular point on the timeline of
human history is our own unique, God-given gift of time on
earth — and it is both our mission and our desire to embrace it
gratefully, responsibly and wholeheartedly. For this very reason we a need the healthy balance that remembering and con-
templating our history can provide. Only in claiming our *whole*
story can we become keenly aware of God's power at work in
the realities of everyday life.

And so we conclude this primer of Spiritual Geography,

with a brief backward glance at the land of the Bible as perceived by some whose lives were profoundly influenced by it. While this is merely a sketchy review, it may move the reader to search out his or her own spiritual genealogy in Sacred Scripture. For it is in God's Holy Word that we come to recognize our true identity and destiny. It's all there in the Bible — our own story, complete and unabridged — God's Word to us, for us and about us.

Like countless numbers before us, we journey through the Bible as *Pilgrims* and as *Pioneers* and discover life's ultimate meaning revealed to us in overlapping stages of the land: (1) The Unknown Land, (2) The Promised Land, and (3) The Holy Land.

The Unknown Land

It had been Abram's father, Terah, who initiated the migration of his family from the cradle of civilization in Mesopotamia to the land of Canaan. But having reached the northernmost arc of the Fertile Crescent, Terah decided to settle there in Haran where he lived for his remaining years (Gn 11:27-32). The journey of his family continued with the call of his son, Abram.

Following the Lord's direction to leave the land of his kinsfolk and go "to a land that I will show you," Abram — together with his wife Sarai, their family, and all their possessions — came to the land of Canaan (Gn 12:1-5). At that time this was the name of the land lying between Syria and Egypt. Abram and Sarai traveled through the land as far as Shechem where the Lord appeared to Abram and said, "To your descendants I will give this land" (Gn 12:7). Abram built an altar there, before moving on through the hill country to Bethel where he erected another altar and invoked God's name. Then, we are told, "Abram journeyed on by stages to the Negeb" (Gn 12:9). Because of a famine there, he sojourned in Egypt for a time, then returned to the land of Canaan. Again the Lord spoke to Abram: "Set forth and walk about in the land, through its length and breadth, for to you I will give it" (Gn 13:17). So Abram and his family settled there, pitching their tents at Hebron where Abram built another altar to the Lord.

Thus, in little more than two short chapters at the very beginning of recorded biblical history, we are introduced to the basic theme of the entire Bible and the story of our life. It is the story of our homeward pilgrimage to the God who all the while journeys with us. This story is one of continuity with our origins and of our faith-pursuit of the dreams and goals initiated by God within our hearts. It reminds us that we belong to one another and that we travel together on this road which takes us through the land's varied terrains. From its very outset our story teaches respect for individual differences in human ideals, talents, needs and preferences and strongly implies that this kind of respect is fundamental to peaceful living. One early example occurs when quarreling breaks out between the herdsmen of Abram and those of his nephew, Lot, because the portion of the land they shared had become too small to accommodate both families:

So Abram said to Lot: "Let there be no strife between

you and me, or between your herdsmen and mine, for we are kinsmen. Is not the whole land at your disposal? Please separate from me. If you prefer the left, I will go to the right; if you prefer the right, I will go to the left." (Gn 13:8, 9)

In other words, this land belongs neither to you nor to me. Rather, we belong to the land. And this land — this life — belongs to God who puts it at our disposal for the journey.

We note, too, that Abram (whose name is later changed to Abraham) acknowledged the Lord at every stage along the way. So shall our story be integrated through prayerful remembering and liturgical celebration of the Lord in our midst and at work in our lives.

The Book of Genesis continues the family history as far as the death of Jacob's son, Joseph, sold into Egypt by his brothers who followed him there in time of famine. "I am about to die," he said to his brothers. "God will surely take care of you and lead you out of this land to the land that he promised on oath to Abraham, Isaac and Jacob" (Gn 50:24).

The Promised Land

While initial migration to the land was Abraham's mission, actual possession of the land was generations away. To bring it about, God worked through such circumstances as the jealousy and evil intent of Joseph's brothers, the cruel oppression of the Hebrews by Egypt's Pharaoh, and the long, arduous trek of the people led by Moses through the desert. We are able enough to identify with these painful situations through corresponding experiences in our own lives. But fathoming the "why?" of such trials and tribulations is no less perplexing for us than it was for the peoples of biblical times: Why do such things happen? Why does God allow this evil in my life? Joseph's loving forgiveness of his brothers provides us with an answer worthy of our meditation: "Even though you meant harm to me, God meant it for good, to achieve his present end, the survival of many people" (Gn 50:20).

It was not in God's plan for Moses to lead the chosen people into the Promised Land but only to its very edge where he could climb the heights and see from a distance that it was within sight:

> This is the land I swore to Abraham, Isaac and Jacob that I would give to their descendants. I have let you feast your eyes upon it, but you shall not cross over. (Dt 34:4)

For Moses it was enough. His eyes had been privileged to behold the land that was already sacred because it was the promise and the gift of God (Dt 32:48-52).

Following the Lord's directive, Moses had prepared Joshua for the next stage of the journey — to cross the Jordan River and lead the people of God into the Promised Land (Dt 31:7,8). The remaining stages would climax with King David capturing the stronghold of Jerusalem and bringing the Ark of the Covenant into that city (2 S 6) — and with Solomon, his son, building the Temple as a fitting dwelling place for the Ark (1 K 5:15-19).

Thus God's promises were fulfilled and it was in this land

that the Israelites could now realize their peoplehood, observe the Covenant and worship their God. How they lived up to these hopes is told in the remainder of the Hebrew Scriptures by people of the land — men and women who were historians, prophets and sages, poets, musicians and storytellers.

The Holy Land

> But when the fullness of time had come, God sent forth his Son, born of a woman... (Gal 4:4)

The union of divinity and humanity in Jesus Christ took place in the land that was already sacred because it had been set apart by God. But from the moment of Mary's "fiat," the land of promise became the holiest place on earth — the Holy Land.

Restoration of Israel by God's Anointed One is a consistent and developing theme throughout the ancient Scriptures. Jesus came in fulfillment of those Scriptures, born into the human family at a time in Jewish history when expectation of the promised Messiah was high. But "...the world did not know him. He came to his own, yet his own people did not accept him" (Jn 1:10, 11). Even John the Baptist acknowledged: "I confess I did not know him, though the reason why I came baptizing with water was that he might be made known to Israel" (Jn 1:31).

The rejection of Jesus by his own people harks back to the story of Joseph (a type of Christ) and his theological interpretation of his brothers' rejection of him: "God meant it for good, to achieve his present end, the survival of many people" (Gn 50:20). Many centuries later in Romans 9-11, Saint Paul would eloquently expand this simple statement into his theological understanding of the non-acceptance of Jesus by his own people. This exposition of God's universal love and mercy rewards our careful attention in ways that can make a difference in our own lives and in our dealings with others. In it, Paul admonishes: "rather than being proud, you should stand in awe" (11:20) — for the Jews remain God's special possession, while we are shoots grafted in their place and supported by the root tree of Judaism (11:17, 18). On the other hand, Paul points to the most awesome confirmation for us of God's irrevocable choice of the Jews: despite their disbelief, "from them came (Jesus) the Messiah" (9:5) in fulfillment of the promises. Ironically, it was the unbelief of Israel that, by God's mercy, opened the door of Christian faith to the Gentiles. By the same divine mercy, the Jews "who belong to the olive tree by nature will be grafted back into their own tree" (11:24). "For God has consigned all to disobedience so that he may show mercy to all" (11:32). A careful reading of Romans 9-11 brings us to Paul's own reflective conclusion:

> Oh, the depth and richness of God's wisdom and
> knowledge! How unfathomable are his judgments,
> how inscrutable his ways! (Rm 11:33)

On the natural level, the most obvious explanation for the rejection of Jesus by the Jews is that he was so human, such an ordinary inhabitant of the land. Was he not, after all, the carpenter's son? And did not everyone know his mother, Mary? (Mt 13:54-58) Likeable people, to be sure, and good neighbors who revered God and raised the boy according to Torah. True, this Jesus became a respected rabbi with a compelling gift of preaching — but still, what he had to say did not always make sense to them: *You must die if you want to live* (cf. Mk 8:35); *To be poor is to be rich* (cf. Mt 5:3); *Be glad when you are excluded, insulted and denounced* (cf. Lk 6:22); *The first among you must serve the rest* (cf. Mk 10:43-45). To a people increasingly impatient with the inequities of their political situation, such talk was hardly of a Messianic nature. In fact, it was not long before the people of his native town "rejected him" (Mt 13:57).

But Jesus moved from town to town proclaiming the kingdom of God and teaching its values in homespun parables. He became known throughout the land which often served as his dwelling — where he stayed and ate and took his rest. The land became the school in which he taught and the visual aid that reinforced his instructions. This land that he loved was an inspiration for his own spirituality as well as for his preaching of the kingdom to others. And when there was need to escape the crowds for a time to commune with the Father in solitude, it was the land that provided him with his favorite places of prayerful retreat.

Throughout his movement within the land he knew and loved, Jesus was all the while making his way toward Jerusalem (Lk 13:22). For Jerusalem was the focal point of the land and the focal point of his life and mission on earth:

"I must keep traveling today and tomorrow and the next day, because it is unacceptable for a prophet to be killed outside Jerusalem" (Lk 13:33).

From Jerusalem would go forth to the whole world the Good News of the redemptive death and resurrection of Jesus (Lk 24:46,47; Acts 1:8). His story would be remembered and passed on by people of the land: men who were fishermen, farmers, shepherds, woodworkers, tanners and tentmakers. And by women of the land: maidens, mothers and widows, home-makers, caretakers and weavers of cloth, catechists, deaconesses and home-church leaders. So it was that from the land that had produced the ancestral Scriptures came forth a New Testament of God at work in that land.

The Land of Pilgrims

I was moved, seized, gripped by this sacred land. I had so loved the book and here I was gazing at its setting! [M. Joseph Lagrange, OP (1855-1938)]

Centuries of Holy Land pilgrims have felt this same magnetic attraction at their first sight of the land that produced the Bible. It was because of the Bible they had come to the land at all. Now it was the land that engaged their senses and henceforth would change the way they would read and understand The Book.

There is something timeless about that small piece of land that speaks to the human heart and mind. Because of the many contrasts of old and new squeezed into meager boundaries, one glance alone sweeps through history and a few steps can bridge civilizations. A momentary lapse of identity is not surprising: Am I a space-age person reaching back to the roots of my earthly beginnings? Or am I, rather, an ancient mortal feeling lost in modern surroundings that are strange and incomprehensible? In truth, I am both.

People of faith cannot separate this experience from the beliefs by which they live. For them the timelessness of the land becomes an overwhelming sense of its holiness. Their feet follow in the footsteps of Jesus and retrace the wilderness route of the Exodus. Their backward glance connects them to a long faith-line of people whose distance from them in time seems somehow diminished. In the setting of this land, descendants and ancestors meet and stand together at the very threshold of their Creator God.

Land of Pioneers

After the destruction of Jerusalem in AD 70, the land of Palestine (as it was then called) remained under changing foreign domination until 1948 when it became the modern state of Israel. Throughout this two thousand year period, the land had been laid to ruin by warring conquerors and subsequent neglect.

In Europe during the nineteenth century, a movement known as Zionism evolved, developed and rapidly spread to Jews dispersed throughout the world. This movement gave birth to their determination to work for the restoration of their devastated land and for the revival of national Jewish life.

Through a series of *aliyahs* (Hebrew term meaning "ingatherings"), large-scale immigration of Jews to Palestine took place. Arriving in the land that Mark Twain had described as "desolate and unlovely... a hopeless, dreary, heart-broken land," these Jews became the pioneers of modern-day Israel in the making. With single-minded resolve they set about to rebuild and transform the land. In the process, it was the land that transformed and rebuilt them into a people. This double impact of the people upon the land and of the land upon the people is captured in the lively tune sung by the Zionist pioneers as they went about their work each day: "To the land we've come, to build and be built by it." The lyrics are an apt description of our experience, too, as we travel as pilgrims and pioneers through the land of our life in the Bible.

Epilogue

Go and do whatever you have in mind for the LORD is
with you. (2 S 7:3)

We must return now with Jesus, in the power of the Spirit,
to our own land of Galilee. The territory is familiar for we have
been pilgrims here all our lives. We walk with assurance on well
worn roads made by others and feel a sense of oneness with
those who went this way before.

But we are pioneers as well as pilgrims, so we discover new
ways to travel the land and create our own paths in unchartered
directions. The journey now lacks clear vision but grips us as
never before with the stronger motivation of a dream that beck-
ons, a mission that calls.

Crossroads appear that challenge us with choices and decisions that must be made if the quest is to continue. At these
junctures we learn to rely on experience and to seek the wisdom of others — but, finally, to subject these helps to our own
heart's counsel.

What, after all, is more dependable than one's own con-
science? For prayerful awareness of God's Spirit moving our
hearts enables us to rightly discern our intuitions and inspira-

tions and to follow these with secure trust in their Divine Source. "Most of all," we are counseled by Sirach 37:15, "pray to God to set your feet in the path of truth."

There are times when the terrain changes suddenly and dramatically, leaving us fearful, doubtful, feeling lost and alone. Most often, these become the times of our greatest growth and conversion. They are the planting seasons in our land when the seed of who we are is sown in the earth to be transformed into the fullness of the person created by God. "Amen, amen, I say to you, if the grain of wheat that falls to the ground does not die, it remains alone; but if it dies, it bears much fruit" (Jn 12:24).

Go now to *your* Galilee. And when you are there, remember and recall what he said and how he lived, what he taught and preached, the healings and miracles he has performed in your land. Go back to his roots, go back to your roots, and discover — for the first time or anew — the Lord Jesus walking along with you on the journey of your life.

May the eyes of your hearts be enlightened.
(Ephesians 1:18)

Galilee Prayer

Lord, Jesus,
You go before me to lead the way.
You walk beside me that I may not lose the way.
You remain with me always because you are The Way.

Jesus of Galilee, dear Jesus of my Galilee,
Let me come to know you more truly in the Gospel.
Let me experience your presence in the land of my life.
Let me discover my own story in yours as together
    we journey to Jerusalem and home.

Amen! Alleluia!